This rock once was mud that hardened and cracked when it was dried by sunshine. The rock now lies near a trail in Glacier National Park, Montana.

Rocks

and their stories

by Carroll Lane Fenton and
Mildred Adams Fenton

Doubleday & Company, Inc.
Garden City, New York

Contents

About Names and Illustrations

Many rocks and most minerals have no everyday English names. Because they don't, scientists have borrowed names from other languages or have made them from Greek and Latin words. Pronunciations of these unfamiliar names are given in the Index, on pages 110–12.

In descriptions, the names of kinds or species as well as those of important groups of rocks and minerals are printed in capital letters, like THIS. Varieties, members of groups, structures, and so on are in *italics*. Pages on which illustrations appear are given in parentheses. "Sandstone (page 54)," for example, means that the illustration of sandstone is on page 54.

Photographs of lignite, anthracite, and bituminous coal were supplied by the Bureau of Mines. Other photographs were made outdoors and from specimens in the collections of the United States National Museum, Princeton University, and Rutgers University. Professors Edward Sampson and Helgi Johnson, and Mr. James Benn, helped us select these specimens.

Among cliffs like these we may find two or three kinds of lava as well as agates and petrified wood.

Let's Collect Rocks

When we hike or go riding in the country, we see rocks of various kinds. Many are pebbles which we find beside roads or in the banks of streams. Some are large boulders that lie in fields, and others are solid ledges of stone to be seen on hillsides or in quarries. Many rocks form steep cliffs, narrow ridges, and mountains with bare, sharp peaks.

Would you like to know more about these rocks and the stories they have to tell? The best way to do this, of course, is to make a collection. At first it will contain interesting stones which you pick up near your home. Later you will add specimens found on trips to mines and quarries, to mountains, or to the seashore. You may also trade specimens with other collectors, or buy specially good ones from dealers. Each piece will be different from the others, and each one will tell its own story about things that have happened to the earth.

Long before your collection becomes very large, you probably will be puzzled by the words *rock* and *stone*. In everyday language, they have about the same meaning. For example, we sometimes call a boulder a big rock, and sometimes call it a stone. We talk about stone buildings or rock walls made to keep banks from sliding. We also read about precious "stones" such as ruby, topaz and diamond.

This is good enough for everyday language, but when we

collect rocks, we have to be more careful with words. We find that precious "stones" really are minerals; they belong to the group of substances from which most rocks are formed. We also find that rocks are not just pebbles, boulders or blocks built into walls. Rocks really are large natural deposits that form part of the earth's outer portion, or "crust." These deposits may be hard, like limestone and granite. They also may be soft or loose, like beds of sand and gravel. Some rocks, such as lava, are hot and molten at one stage of their existence. Later they cool and become very hard.

But if rocks are all these things, what are stones?

Stone is a word that has two meanings, and we need both of them. According to one meaning, stones are rocks that are solid and hard enough to form ledges, blocks and boulders. Granite, for example, is both a rock and this kind of stone. Limestone and sandstone also are stones, for they are deposits of rock material that have become solid and hard.

Stone, then, may be hard rock. But we still need a word for pieces or rock that range from pebbles to big boulders. Since these pieces are hard and stony, we may call them stones. If we are careful to show that they are pieces, not deposits, people will know what we mean.

Well, that's enough about words. Let's now pick up some specimens and find out what they tell about rocks and the things of which they are made.

Rocks and Their Minerals

Can you find a rock like the one in the picture on page 10? It shows why we say that rocks—*most* rocks—are made up of minerals.

This particular specimen is granite. It began as part of a huge, hot, soft mass far down inside the earth. In time the hot mass cooled and hardened. As it did so, various materials in it separated into crystals, thin scales, and grains. We give these materials the name of *minerals.*

How much difference is there between a rock and a mineral? About as much as the difference between a fruit cake and the flour, sugar or dried fruit that are used to make it. Each of them is a separate substance, but they make up one cake. Minerals in our granite are separate substances, too, but all of them together form one rock.

There is another way in which minerals resemble the materials, or ingredients, in a cake. When a baker mixes so much of each ingredient with the others, he makes a certain kind of cake. If he leaves out some things and adds others, he has a cake of a different kind. If he changes materials still more, he may not have cake at all. Instead, he will have sweet rolls or raisin bread. Yet all these will contain such ingredients as flour, sugar and raisins.

The same thing happens when kinds and proportions of minerals change. One variety of granite is pale and coarse.

Four minerals make up this granite, which is a rock.

It contains only two minerals, feldspar and quartz. The granite shown on this page contains these and two others. They produce a variety that is darker and more grainy than the one with only two minerals.

Let's now look at the three rocks shown on page 12. Diorite looks rather like our specimen of granite. We find that it contains the same minerals, but in different proportions. Syenite contains feldspar, amphibole, mica, and some other things, but no quartz; it does not look quite so much like granite. The third rock, anorthosite, is still more different from granite. We are not surprised to find that it contains feldspar but no quartz, amphibole or mica. Their places are taken by small amounts of pyroxene and magnetite. These minerals are not found in the other rocks.

But are all rocks made of minerals? And do these minerals always form mixtures of two or more kinds?

We can answer the second question by looking at a piece of rock salt. It is white or pale gray and is formed by one mineral—salt. If other minerals are present, they are unimportant impurities. Rock salt would be just about the same without them. Gypsum, sulphur and pure varieties of limestone also are rocks made of one mineral.

Coal and some other substances show that rocks are not always made up of minerals. Coal is a rock that forms deposits as much as forty feet in thickness. Yet it consists of material that once was part of living, growing plants. The only minerals in coal are impurities that were mixed with the plant material.

When you collect rocks you will get specimens of coal, rock salt, sulphur and the purest varieties of limestone. You also will want specimens of rock-making minerals. At first you will name, or identify, these minerals by comparing them with pictures. Soon, however, you will find specimens which do not look quite like the pictures in this or any other book. You will also find minerals that look alike in pictures but really are quite different.

Such minerals must be identified by comparing them with descriptions. These give the color, weight, appearance, and so on, and most of them need no explanation. You can easily tell whether a specimen is pink, black, or some other color. You also can see the shape of its crystals, and can tell whether it is light or heavy just by "hefting" it. Two things that may not be so clear, however, are streak and the numbers for hardness.

Streak is the color a mineral makes when it is rubbed against the back of a tile or some other piece of unglazed "porcelain." This color often is very different from the

Feldspar
Quartz
Mica
Amphibole
Diorite
Feldspar
Amphibole
Mica
Other Minerals
Syenite
Feldspar
Magnetite
Pyroxene
Anorthosite

color of the entire specimen. Some blackish minerals, for example, make dark red streaks, and some green, purple and blue minerals make white streaks. These may be much more important than the color of grains or crystals.

Hardness is something we can feel. The only way to measure it, however, is to find out what minerals scratch other things or can be scratched by them. The softest mineral can be scratched by your fingernail; we measure its hardness as 1. The hardest mineral, which is diamond, scratches all the others; its hardness is said to be 10. Here is the scale from 1 to 8, with an example of each hardness:

1. Scratched easily by your fingernail; the mineral feels soft and greasy. (Talc)
2. Barely scratched by your fingernail, but does not feel soft. (Gypsum)
3. Barely scratched by a sharp piece of copper, such as the edge of a new penny. (Calcite)
4. Scratched easily by a knife, but not by a penny. (Fluorite)
5. Barely scratched by a knife. (Apatite)
6. Scratches a knife and may barely scratch glass. (Feldspar)
7. Scratches glass easily, and is harder than any other common substance. (Quartz)
8. Scratches quartz easily, but is not common. (Topaz)

A knife, a penny, and some small pieces of gypsum, calcite, apatite, feldspar and quartz will do for your determinations of hardness. Add some "porcelain" tiles like those used in floors or on bathroom walls and you will be ready to identify the minerals that make up rocks.

Knowing the Minerals

Most of us start our collections with three minerals. One is colorless, white, red or brown. It scratches glass and is sometimes made into "shooter" marbles. The second mineral is colorless or white, is just scratched by a penny, and bubbles when acid is dropped on it. The third mineral is yellowish, looks like metal, and will scratch a knife. It often forms shiny blocks that are very brittle.

Can you identify these minerals from the following descriptions and pictures?

This will not be as hard to do as you may think. There are more than eleven hundred kinds of minerals in the world, and about four hundred varieties. Only a few of these, however, are so plentiful that we call them rock-makers, or rock-making minerals. A few more are so useful or so interesting that you will want to know about them and get specimens for your collection.

This means that only about forty kinds and varieties of minerals need to be described in this book. Most of these are so different from the rest that you can identify them easily. Except for a few varieties, descriptions are arranged in alphabetical order. This arrangement will help you look up the various minerals when you find their names on specimens or in descriptions of rocks.

Agate (page 15) is a variety of quartz that is clouded or

A banded agate from Brazil.

striped with different colors produced by impurities. These colors range from white to gray, green, orange-red or brown. Agates have a hardness of 7; broken pieces scratch a knife easily. The mineral looks either glassy or waxy and can be brightly polished.

Agates are found in many places, but the finest striped ones come from Brazil. Water in the ground made them by filling holes in lava with thin layers of quartz. Although the layers were hard, the water was able to soak through them and deposit still more quartz, until the holes were filled. Often the last deposit consisted of tiny, colorless crystals.

Since many natural agates are dull, people color them with heat and chemicals. When most brown agates are heated they turn red and look like the natural ones called *carnelians.* Chemicals in which banded agates are soaked generally do not affect some layers but stain others red, black, or even blue. These stained layers show plainly in polished specimens.

AMPHIBOLE (page 17) is the name of a group of minerals with colors that range from white to dark green, brown or black. Most amphiboles look satiny or glassy; their hardness is 5 to 6, and the streak is paler than the mineral. Crystals may be blunt and six-sided or they may be thin needles. Amphiboles are rare in hardened lavas, but are common in rocks of the granitic group and in others called metamorphic. Dark amphibole may look so much like dark pyroxene that you will not be able to tell them apart.

APATITE (page 27) generally is white, green or brown, with a white streak. The mineral is brittle, has a hardness of 5, and looks glassy. Apatite is common in many kinds of rocks, but its crystals generally are too small to be seen. Some crystals, however, are very large.

Asbestos (page 18) is a variety of the mineral serpentine. Asbestos looks satiny, and its hardness is between 2 and 3. White, brown and yellowish brown are the commonest colors. Asbestos can be pulled into threadlike fibers which bend easily. Since these fibers resist heat, they are used in fireproof materials and in other things that become very hot. Asbestos is mined in Arizona and the Canadian province of Quebec, as well as in southern Africa. The mineral name for this material is *chrysotile*.

CALCITE (page 20) is the most important mineral in limestone and is found in many other rocks. When pure it is colorless to white; the colorless type is translucent. Impurities produce colors such as yellow, pink, green or pale brown; the streak is colorless. Calcite is bright or glassy in appearance and has a hardness of 3. When weak acid is dropped on it, the mineral bubbles, or effervesces.

Calcite forms crystals of various shapes, all of which can be split into blocks that seem to have been "squashed" sidewise. Most calcite, however, consists of tiny irregular bits which show no crystalline structure. The best way to identify this form of calcite is to put some acid on it and watch it bubble.

Feldspar

Feldspar

Dolomite

Epidote

Amphibole

Copper

Asbestos, or chrysotile, is a fibrous mine

Iceland spar is colorless, transparent calcite. If you can get a block at least a half inch thick, lay it on this page. You will see that the letters appear twice, though they may overlap. This is called *double refraction*.

Dogtooth spar is calcite in long, sharp-pointed crystals. *Satin spar* consists of thin, straight fibers which give the mineral a satiny appearance. This name also is used for a satiny variety of gypsum.

COPPER (page17; often called "native" copper) is the only pure metal that is common in rocks. It forms flakes and irregular lumps or nuggets, some of which are very large. These nuggets are generally covered with dull material, but under it is the dark red metal we see in pennies, electric wires, and many other things. The hardness is between 2 and 3. Copper is heavy and bends easily.

DOLOMITE (page 17) looks much like calcite, but is harder (almost 4) and forms fewer kinds of crystals. It also does not bubble when cold acid is dropped on it, but will "fizz" if the acid is hot. Like calcite, dolomite is more common as small particles and grains than it is in the form of crystals. Colors range from white to pink or buff, and are caused by impurities. The streak is colorless.

EPIDOTE (page 17) is a very common mineral, especially in rocks that have been changed by heat and mountain-building. It generally forms small particles that are yellowish green in color, but crystals are thin and dark green or almost black. The streak is white and the hardness 6 to 7.

FELDSPAR (page 17) is the name of a group of minerals that look very much alike. They form blocks or blocklike crystals which also split into smooth-sided blocks. Pale yellow, pink, red and gray are the commonest colors; green, brown and dark olive-gray are not so common. The streak is white and the hardness is about 6. Fresh surfaces generally look glassy or pearly. Weathered pieces may resemble calcite, but acid never makes them bubble.

Feldspars are the most abundant of all mineral groups; quartz and calcite come next. There are several kinds and varieties of feldspar, with names such as *orthoclase, microcline* and *plagioclase.* Some of these form crystals as much as twenty feet thick. A beautiful green variety that is polished for gems is known as *Amazon stone.*

FLUORITE (page 22) is Number 4 in the scale of hardness. Crystals generally are cubes, but coarse grains are more common. Green, purple and deep yellow are the colors most often found. Fluorite is used in steel, glass, and enamels for such things as stoves and refrigerators.

GALENA (page 22) is the most important and commonest mineral containing lead. Galena forms brittle cubes that split into smaller cubes. The color and streak are lead gray; the hardness is between 2 and 3, and the weight is almost as great as the weight of copper. Many good crystals are found, but most of the galena in lead ore forms coarse grains.

GRAPHITE is the mineral used in making "lead" pencils. It is pure carbon in the form of grains, scales, flakes, or

Calcite crystals (dogtooth spar) and a block of calcite (Iceland spar) that shows double refraction.

thin, flat crystals. Graphite is soft (hardness 1 to 2) and is light in weight. It feels greasy and can be bent. The color is steel gray or black, and the streak is grayish black and shiny. Graphite is found in many rocks that have been changed when they were crumpled into mountains.

GYPSUM (page 21) is white, yellowish or colorless, with a white streak. Its hardness is 2. Although it may look like calcite, it never bubbles when acid is dropped on it.

Selenite is a variety that forms platy masses and flat crystals which often are arranged in pairs. They split in three directions; thin pieces can be bent but do not come back into shape. *Satin spar* is fibrous and shiny, like satin. It is softer than the variety of calcite called by the same name, and does not bubble in acid. *Desert roses* form in dry regions, where water dissolves gypsum and then deposits it in clusters of plates that look like flowers. These often are colored by clay or hematite.

Rock gypsum is grainy and massive, and forms beds of stone. Impurities generally stain it gray, brown or pink. Rock gypsum is softer than limestone, dissolves easily, and does not bubble when you drop acid on it. Great amounts of this rock are used in plasters of various kinds, in cement, and in fertilizer. Even the "chalk" used in school is made from gypsum.

HEMATITE (page 24) is often called "red iron ore." Its commonest variety is grainy, dull, and dark red in color. The streak is brighter red, the hardness is about 6, and the weight is greater than that of most minerals. *Red ochre* is a crumbly, earthy variety that forms beds and also is found in some concretions. *Kidney ore* is solid and dark red; it forms dark lumps that resemble kidneys, though the mineral looks fibrous when it is broken. *Specular hematite* consists of small crystals and plates. They are iron-black but shine with a bright metallic luster.

Clinton ore is beds or layers of hematite that settled in ancient seas. Some is grainy, or oolitic; some contains shells and other fossils, and is called "fossil ore." *Lake Superior ore* is red or reddish brown, and may be either hard or crumbly. It was formed when water dissolved some of the material from rocks containing iron minerals, which were changed into hematite. Enormous amounts of this ore have been mined near Lake Superior.

HORNBLENDE is a common, dark-colored mineral belonging to the amphibole group.

Crystals of gypsum (variety selenite) and a desert rose.

Fluorite

Galena

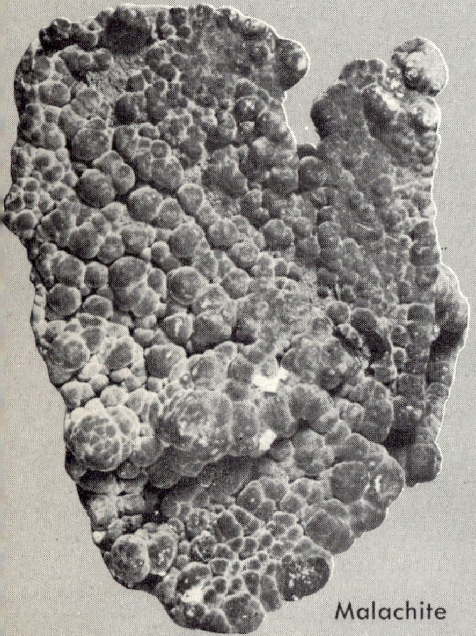

Malachite

Pyrite, or "Fool's Gold"

Biotite, or Black Mica

Muscovite,
or White Mica

LIMONITE (page 24) is an iron mineral that often looks like rust, and contains the same substances. Limonite does not form crystals, but it may be hard and metallic. It also forms masses that look fibrous when they are broken, much as kidney ore does. Limonite is yellow, brown or black; its streak is yellowish brown; its hardness is about 5 but less than 6. *Yellow ochre* is a soft, earthy variety. *Bog iron* is limonite mixed with clay and other material; it still is forming in swamps. In Europe, limonite is an important iron ore.

MAGNETITE (page 24) is also called magnetic iron ore. It forms coarse grains or shiny crystals that are steel gray to black in color. The streak is black and the hardness ranges from about 5 to more than 6. The name magnetite comes from the fact that this mineral is held by a magnet, just as iron is. *Lodestone* is a variety that is magnetic; a piece of it will hold nails and other things made of iron.

Magnetite deposits are important iron ores in New York, New Jersey, Pennsylvania, Europe and Brazil.

MALACHITE (page 22) is a rich green mineral containing copper; its streak is light green. Malachite forms crusts, velvety tufts, and kidney-shaped masses. The hardness is 4 or a little less. This mineral makes beautiful specimens and is often polished for ornaments. Most malachite now comes from Africa, though many fine specimens have been found in Arizona.

MICA (page 22) is a convenient name for a group of minerals that split into very thin sheets. These sheets can be bent, but when we let them go they become flat again. Mica forms thin scales and flat, six-sided crystals with rough sides. The luster is glassy, the streak is white, and the hardness is only 2 to 3.

Muscovite, or white mica, is transparent and generally has no color, though it may be greenish or brownish. *Biotite*

Limonite

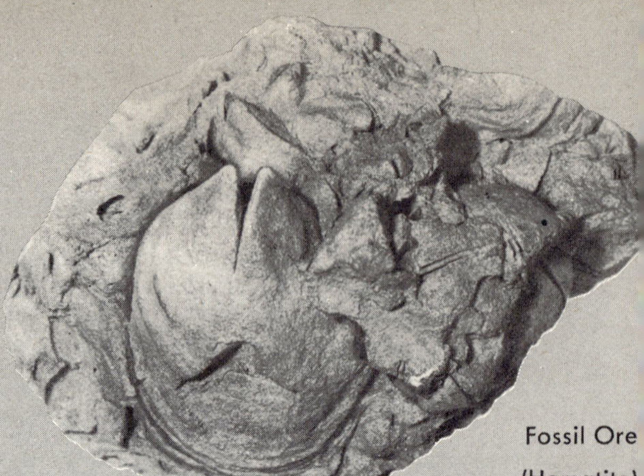

Fossil Ore (Hematite)

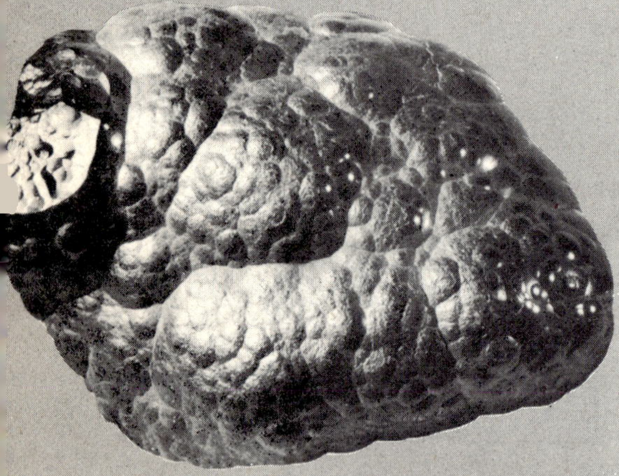

Kidney Ore (Hematite)

Fibrous Limonite

Specular Hematite

Magnetite, or Magnetic Iron Ore

(black mica) is black, dark brown, or deep green. Both muscovite and biotite are found in rocks of the granitic group, but only biotite is common in hardened lavas. Muscovite is used for electrical insulation, as well as for movie "snow" and various other purposes.

PYRITE (page 22) is commonly called "fool's gold" because people who don't know minerals sometimes mistake it for true gold. Pyrite is bright, metallic, brassy yellow, but its streak is greenish black. Crystals generally are box-shaped and often have fine lines across their sides. The hardness is 6 or more. Pyrite is found in rocks of many kinds, from coal to limestone and even granite.

PYROXENE (page 27) is the name for a group of minerals which contain magnesium. Some are white, but brown, dark green, and black are the commonest colors. The streak is white to grayish green, and the hardness is 5 to 6. Some pyroxenes are dull but others are glassy or resinous, and all of them are brittle. Crystals often are small and short, with eight sides and blunt pyramids at each end. Pyroxenes are commonest in dark-colored rocks that once were molten.

QUARTZ (page 26) is the most abundant *single* mineral in rocks, though all the feldspars together are more plentiful. Pure quartz is colorless or white, but impurities give the mineral pink, purple, brown and other colors. The streak is white or very light colored. Although quartz forms beautiful six-sided crystals, large deposits are massive or grainy. It has a hardness of 7, looks glassy, and is brittle. Instead of splitting, like calcite and feldspar, it breaks in such a way that surfaces resemble shells. This is called *conchoidal* fracture. Crystals commonly have fine lines across their glassy sides.

Quartz mixed with other minerals in rocks often looks gray and rough. *Chalcedony* (page 27) is a variety that

Quartz crystals and a broken piece of rose quartz, a variety named for its delicate rose pink color.

looks waxy. It never crystallizes, but forms layers and masses that sometimes resemble bunches of grapes.

SALT (page 27) can be easily told by its taste. It forms grains and crystals which are cubes and can be split into smaller cubes with shiny sides. Pure salt is colorless and transparent; impurities make it white, gray, yellow, pinkish or brick red. The hardness is 2.5.

The mineral name for salt is HALITE. In many places, halite settled in beds, forming *rock salt.* Some deposits of rock salt are almost four hundred feet thick.

SERPENTINE has two varieties. One is massive and is yellowish green or dark green in color. It has a white streak and looks waxy but cannot be split into sheets. Its hardness is 3 or a little less. The second variety forms fibers and is generally called *asbestos* (page 18). You will find a description of it under that name.

SULPHUR (page 27) forms bright yellow masses and crystals that are brilliant or resemble resin. The streak is white or pale yellow and the hardness is about 2. Crystals are brittle, but some masses can be cut with a knife. The mineral melts easily and burns with a blue flame.

Sulphur

Salt Crystals, or Halite

Tourmaline

Apatite

Pyroxene

Topaz

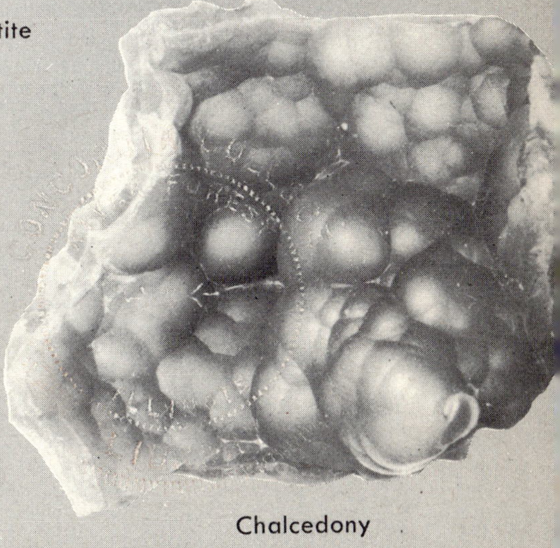

Chalcedony

Sulphur often forms in volcanoes; during ancient times it also settled in shallow seas. There it formed impure beds. Deposits of rock sulphur, 125 feet in thickness, lie deep down in the ground under parts of Louisiana and Texas. Sulphur is used in rubber, fertilizer, matches, and many other things.

TALC is Number 1 in our scale of hardness. It seldom forms crystals, but is found in masses that can be split into scales or thin, wavy sheets. The color is yellow, green or gray, and the streak is white. Fresh pieces look and feel greasy or soapy.

Pure talc is ground up to make talcum powder. It also is used in paper, rubber, roofing, linoleum, and many other things. Thick deposits of this mineral are called soapstone.

TOPAZ (page 27) is a rare mineral which often is cut into gems. You will be interested in it because it is Number 8 in the scale of hardness. Topaz forms masses and brilliant crystals that split crosswise. Some are colorless, but others are white, yellow, brown or blue; yellow topaz becomes pink when it is heated. Worn pieces resemble pebbles of quartz, but are much harder.

TOURMALINE (page 27) forms crystals with grooves running lengthwise along their sides. The ends have blunt points or are almost flat. Black is the commonest color, but some crystals are green, brown, pink or even blue. The streak is white and the hardness is 7 or more. Both crystals and broken surfaces look glassy. Tourmaline is common in very coarse-grained granite and several other kinds of rock.

Tales Told by Lava

One winter day in 1943, a Mexican farmer named Polido was plowing in his cornfield. Suddenly the ground shook and began to crack. Out came clouds of steam and cinders. Then large, hot stones shot up into the air.

The farmer stopped plowing and ran to the village. "There's a fire monster in the ground!" he told people. "It is breathing out steam, ashes and stones that are falling upon my field!"

Polido's "fire monster" really was a new volcano. It was made by hot rock called lava, which had formed as a "pocket" far below the earth's surface. At first the pocket was not truly molten, but was thick and doughy. In fact, we call such material *magma,* from an ancient word that means "dough." Magma turns into *lava* when it erupts, or comes out of the ground.

Although the magma formed far below the surface, it began to work its way upward. Up . . . up . . . up it went, pushing and eating its way through the rocks that covered it. At last the pocket of magma lay only a few hundred feet under Polido's cornfield.

No one knows just how long this took or exactly how it happened. We do know that the magma became softer and softer as it came nearer and nearer the surface. It also took in, or absorbed, a great deal of water which was turned into steam. The pocket resembled a huge, overheated boiler that was ready to explode.

Explosions came as soon as the ground cracked open. Molten rock was blown into ashes and cinders, which came out of the crack in clouds that looked like black smoke. Steam also blew out lumps of lava which hardened as they sailed through the air. At night those lumps of lava glowed like red balls of fire.

When the cinders and ashes fell to the ground, they built a cone-shaped hill that rapidly grew into a mountain. Lava ran out of cracks in its sides, and flowed from other cracks that opened in the ground. The molten rock covered roads, fields and even buildings before it cooled and turned into stone.

Many people have traveled thousands of miles to see the new volcano that formed in Farmer Polido's cornfield. Still more people visit older volcanoes, lava flows and deposits of ash and cinders to be found in our own country.

This small volcano is a cinder cone. It consists of cinders, or lapilli, which also cover the ground around it.

A bread-crust bomb with a cracked surface and two spindle bombs. All were found at the Craters of the Moon, in Idaho.

Before we examine these things, however, we must check the meaning of two words which we shall want to use.

The first of these words is *igneous;* its original meaning was "fiery." During early times, people thought that smoke and real flames came out of volcanoes. We now know that the "smoke" really is steam mixed with fine ash, while most of the "flames" are only the glow of red-hot or yellow-hot rock. In spite of this, we use the word *igneous* as a name for all rocks that have been either magma or molten lava. All rocks that come from cracks or volcanoes are igneous, and so are many others that hardened underground.

Another useful word is *eruptive.* All igneous rocks that come out of cracks or volcanoes erupt, and therefore may be called eruptive. They also may be called *extrusive.* Both words have about the same meaning, and both help us tell igneous rocks that came to the surface while they were hot from those that hardened and cooled deep down in the earth.

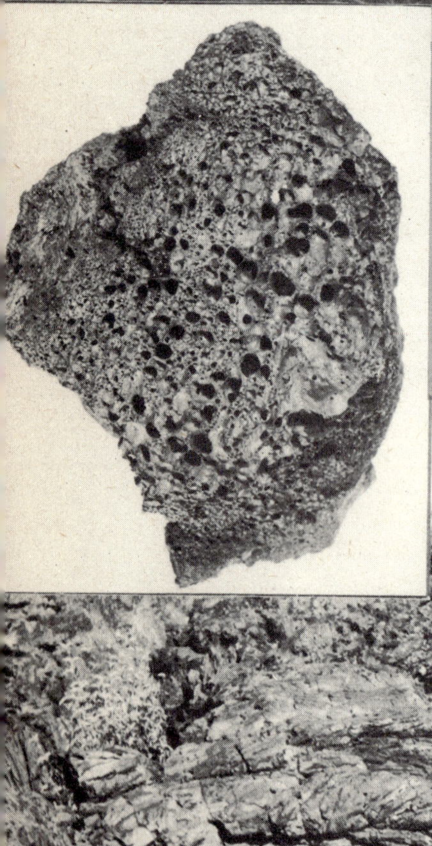

The upper picture shows the edge of a flow o blocky lava in Lassen Volcanic National Park California. At the left is a piece of scoria. Th lower picture shows ropy structure in a lav flow at the Craters of the Moon, Idaho. A these consist of the dark eruptive rock calle basalt.

Lava is an eruptive rock—but that's not the end of our story. In coming to the surface and hardening, it takes on various forms and structures. Here are the most important, with descriptions to help you recognize them and tell how they formed:

VOLCANIC ASH. This is not true ash, since it has not been burned. It actually is once-molten lava that was blown into tiny pieces by explosive eruptions. The pieces then cooled and hardened very quickly. Volcanic ash may be white, gray, brown, purplish, or almost black. White ash generally contains a great deal of quartz, but dark ash contains more iron. When dark volcanic ash is weathered it makes very rich soil.

CINDERS, or LAPILLI, are pieces of exploded lava which may be as big as walnuts or as small as peas. They are full of tiny holes, or bubbles, made when steam swelled up as the molten rock exploded. Most cinders are dark, though some are light colored. Northeast of Crater Lake, in Oregon, you may find pale yellow cinders which are so full of bubbles that they float on water.

BOMBS (page 31) may be almost as small as cinders, or they may be several feet thick. Most bombs began as lumps of soft lava that were tossed out of volcanoes, and hardened as they sailed through the air. Some rolled into smooth balls, but others twisted into shapes that look like pears, half-moons, or cigars. *Bread-crust bombs* are named for their cracked surfaces, which hardened while the lava inside was still soft and was swelling as bread does when it bakes. *Spindle bombs* stretched and twisted as they hardened, and ribbon bombs stretched still more. The best place to find bombs is the surface of a cinder deposit near a small volcano. Bombs appear as larger stones lying upon the cinders.

Lavas that ran out of the ground often are more interesting than bombs, ash and cinders. Here are some things to look for in hardened lava flows:

ROPY STRUCTURE (page 32) is found in lava that was very thin, or "runny." Such lava could flow downhill at speeds of six to eighteen miles per hour, wrinkling and twisting as it went. The wrinkles and twists were preserved as the molten rock hardened. Many ropy lava flows also shine like satin, and therefore look bright in spite of their dark colors. People of Hawaii call ropy lava *pahoehoe.*

BLOCKY LAVA (page 32) was stiff as it came out of the ground. Its surface therefore became hard while its under part kept on flowing. Thus the lava broke into irregular chunks which often tumbled over each other. When the whole flow finally hardened, it formed a dark, rough jumble. People often call such lava flows *malpais,* the Spanish for "bad country," because they are hard to cross. In Hawaii

Columns formed as a lava flow cooled and cracked. These stand beside U. S. Highway 97, south of Ellensburg, Washington.

Layers of ash, cinders and hardened lava in the old volcano that now is partly filled by Crater Lake, Oregon.

they are *aa*.

COLUMNS (page 34) formed in many lava flows as they cooled. Cooling made the rock shrink, and shrinking produced cracks. Three cracks generally ran out from one center, working down deeper and deeper till they reached the bottom of the flow. When cracks came together they divided the lava into columns which often—but not always—have six sides. Some columns are only a few inches across—just right for specimens. Other columns are several feet across and as much as fifty feet tall. The only way to collect such huge things is to take photographs of them.

SCORIA (page 32) is bubbly lava; its holes may be as small as BB shot or they may measure several inches. The holes were made by bubbles of steam which swelled as the molten rock erupted. When the lava hardened, the holes remained, just as they did in cinders. Both ropy and blocky lava may be filled with steam holes, but flows that cracked into columns generally are too solid to be called scoria.

Both lava flows and cinders build volcanoes. Cinders alone make cone-shaped hills or mountains with craters at the top, known as cinder cones. There are great numbers of cinder cones in the western United States and in Mexico. Some are only a few feet high, but others are more than a thousand feet in height.

Volcanoes made of nothing but lava look like gently curved domes. Small ones are not very high, but big ones are many thousands of feet high. The world's largest volcano is a dome-shaped mountain of lava in the Hawaiian Islands. Its slopes are not so steep as many roads.

Most high, steep volcanoes are made of both lava and cinders. About five thousand years ago, one of these steep volcanoes erupted and then collapsed. This produced a huge kettle-shaped depression that now is filled by Crater Lake, in Oregon. If you stand on the rim above Crater Lake, you can see layers of lava and layers of ash and cinders which built up the ancient mountain. You will also see a small cone that was built by eruptions after the mountain fell in.

Rocks that Erupted

When we collect eruptive rocks, we should keep two sets of specimens. One set will show cinders, scoria, bombs, and other forms which lava takes as it comes out of the ground. The other set will show different kinds of eruptive rocks, each one with its own characteristics.

BASALT (page 32) probably is the commonest kind of lava. Freshly broken basalt is dark gray, greenish, purplish or black, though the weathered rock generally is dull brown. Broken surfaces are fine-grained and dull or velvety, but one variety shows small grains of quartz. Basalt may be either solid or porous, it forms blocky, ropy, or solid-looking flows that often crack into columns. The columns may break into curved sections or into thin chips when they are weathered. In dry regions, weathered basalt is often coated with limy material left as water evaporates.

ANDESITE (page 40) is almost as common as basalt. It generally is gray, pink, dull red, or brown, though it may be purplish. Most andesite contains coarse grains or small crystals of minerals. These, and the lighter color, help you tell the rock from basalt. *Dacite* (page 39) is a variety of andesite that generally contains small crystals of feldspar and quartz. The rock may be pink, pale gray, or almost black.

RHYOLITE (page 40) is pink, red, or light brown lava

which often contains crystals of quartz or glassy-looking feldspar. It may also show different-colored bands formed as the lava flowed out upon the ground. Rhyolite probably would have been granite if it had hardened far below the surface, where its minerals could form crystals and grains.

Felsite is a name sometimes used for rhyolite, dacite and andesite. It is useful if you can't tell them apart.

OBSIDIAN (page 40) is volcanic glass. It was stiff when it erupted, and hardened too quickly for separate minerals to form. The commonest color is black, but red and gray obsidian may be found. It is harder than glass and breaks with thin, sharp edges. Indians often chipped obsidian into knives, scrapers, spearheads, and delicate arrow points. Many of these were so fine that the Indians used them only in ceremonies or as offerings to their gods.

Pitchstone (page 40) is a variety of obsidian that looks like tar or resin. Light may be seen through very thin pieces, though thick ones look grainy. *Pumice* (page 40) is obsidian containing so many holes that it looks like froth. Colors range from white to pale yellow, brown, or dull red. This rock weighs so little that it floats on water and is carried long distances by winds. Cinders of pumice from the old volcano now filled by Crater Lake were carried at least eighty miles by the wind. Larger pieces of pumice, erupted from volcanoes on islands, have been known to float upon the ocean for as long as a year and a half.

AGGLOMERATE (page 39) began as a mixture of ash, bombs, and broken stones erupted from cracks or volcanoes. This mixture has been cemented into very coarse stone. Its color depends upon the kind of lava in it. Basalt agglomerate is dark, but agglomerate made of andesite may be gray or pinkish brown. Some rhyolite agglomerate is almost rose colored.

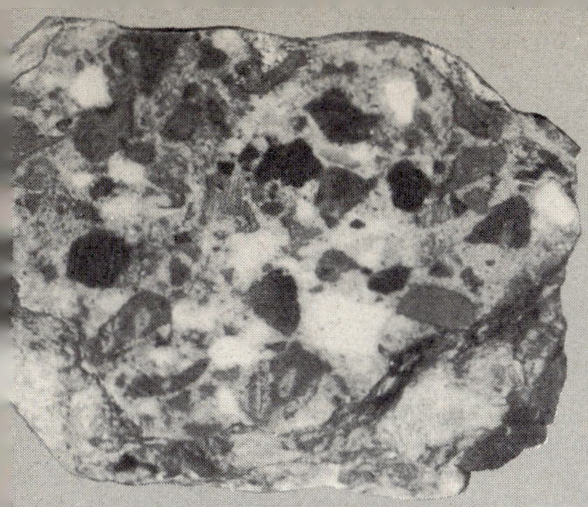

upper picture shows cemented ash bits of stone in a piece of light-red agglomerate.

he right is a weathered cliff of ag-merate beside the road from Cody, oming, to Yellowstone National Park.

large block of light-colored dacite ow) contains darker lumps of the e kind of rock. The whitish dots are dspar crystals.

Tuff

Rhyolite with
Flow Structure

Pitchstone

Pumice

Andesite

Obsidian

TUFF (page 40) is cemented volcanic ash and is white to gray or brown in color. In some deposits the ash is cemented firmly, forming hard stone. Much tuff is rather soft and is full of small holes, or pores. At the Bandelier National Monument, in northern New Mexico, ancient Indians dug their homes in a cliff of porous tuff which contains many chips of obsidian.

Traprock is a name used by quarrymen for dark lava and dark, grainy rocks that hardened underground. Many "traprock" deposits are basalt.

Eruptive rocks are found in many parts of North America, from the Atlantic Coast to the Pacific. Yellowstone National Park is a specially good place to see obsidian, pitchstone and rhyolite. Great cliffs of agglomerate stand on both sides of the road that runs to the park from the town of Cody, Wyoming. Dacite forms Lassen Peak, in California, and several nearby mountains. Mount Rainier, however, consists of tuff and andesite. Beds of tuff near the town of Florissant, Colorado, settled in ancient lakes and contain many fossil leaves. Very fine flows of basalt may be found at the Craters of the Moon, Idaho, and a few miles from Lassen Peak. Others may be seen from roads across Arizona and New Mexico.

Many ancient lava flows in the East have been covered by later formations. Still, fine exposures of columnar basalt may be found in Connecticut, in the Watchung Mountains of New Jersey, and in other regions.

The Granitic Group

Most granite once was hotter than lava, but it cooled and hardened deep underground. Because it did so, it tells a different story. It also became a different type of fiery, or igneous, rock.

Suppose we imagine an ancient pocket of magma, and find out how it turned into granite. The materials in this pocket were not like those that make basalt or andesite. The pocket itself was much bigger than the one that finally erupted through Farmer Polido's cornfield. The granite magma also lay much deeper in the ground. It probably was about thirty miles below the earth's surface.

As year after year went by, the huge mass of doughy rock slowly moved upward. It probably moved from side to side, too. It went where the rocks of the earth's "crust" were weakest, for there it could rise most easily.

At last the magma came to a place where the "crust" was crumpling into mountains. The doughy stuff filled the mountains as they were bent upward. Magma also spread out in irregular sheets and filled great up-and-down cracks.

After this the magma could go no higher, so it cooled and began to harden. We already know how substances in it separated, forming mineral grains and crystals. The grains generally were no bigger than sand or peas, but the crystals sometimes became very large. Those found in one coarse variety of granite are as much as thirty feet long and weigh as much as ninety tons.

Even after the granite cooled and hardened, it lay deep down underground. There it stayed while the mountains above it were worn away. Frost broke the rocks to pieces; rain water that soaked into the ground changed or dissolved their minerals. Swiftly flowing rivers then washed worn rock material to lowlands or the sea. At last the wrinkled rocks disappeared, leaving the grainy granite at the surface of the earth.

Many years ago, geologists thought *all* granite once was doughy magma that hardened underground. Now we say that *most* granite formed in this way. Then we add this explanation to tell how the rest was made:

Some pockets of magma stopped rising before they got very far into the crumpling mountains. The doughy stuff hardened very slowly, for its heat had to go out through all the rocks that covered the magma. They kept the magma from cooling quickly, just as layers of blankets keep you from becoming cold on a winter night.

As heat went upward through the rocks, it changed some of their minerals. In most places, however, heat was not nearly so important as the steam that came with it. This steam worked its way into tiny cracks and pores. As it did so, it dissolved particles of minerals. Then it carried them away as it went through the rocks.

For each particle the steam took away, it left another particle which it had brought from the granite magma. We might say that the steam "exchanged" granite minerals for those in limestone, shale, or other rocks. By keeping up this exchange for many years, the steam remade these other rocks and turned them into granite.

There are great deposits of made-over granite in the east-

Granite shown in the upper picture has been weathered into blocks and columns. Coarse sand that covers the ground came from the crumbling stone.

At the left is a piece of pegmatite containing a large block of feldspar.

Granite shown in the picture below has been weathered into slabs that resemble "courses" of stone in a man-made wall.

ern part of North America. They look almost exactly like granite made when doughy rock cooled under wrinkled mountains. Of course, their minerals did come from hot, doughy magmas. We need not worry if we cannot tell made-over granites from the other sort.

In everyday language, the word *granite* means almost any igneous rock made of coarse grains and crystals. It is much better, however, to say that all these rocks belong to the coarse-grained, or *granitic*, group. This group then may be divided into various kinds and varieties, depending upon their appearance and the minerals they contain.

GRANITE (pages 10, 44 and 47) is the commonest and most important coarse-grained igneous rock. It always contains feldspar and quartz; most granite also contains mica, amphibole, and a few other minerals. They make the rock pale gray, pink, brick red, or even grayish green. The pale gray, buff or pink variety called *graphic granite* contains only feldspar and quartz. The feldspar forms smooth-sided blocks, and quartz fills the spaces between them. Because of this, it has zigzag shapes that resemble some ancient types of writing.

Pegmatite (page 44) is also known as giant granite. It is the variety that contains very large crystals. The one that weighed ninety tons was a crystal of mica. A feldspar crystal was so big it filled two freight cars when it was taken out of the ground. Some deposits of pegmatite also contain holes so large that a man can stand in them.

Granite is a hard, strong rock which is often used in buildings. In spite of this, granite deposits are full of cracks which divide the rock into blocks or slabs. They let water sink into the ground, where it changes minerals. It also freezes when winter comes, pushing against the broken blocks with more force than we can imagine.

Changing, breaking and freezing "weather" the granite. They wear it down into rounded blocks, or divide it into slabs that fit together, almost like stones in walls. Curved slabs also are broken off, forming arches and domes in the rock that remains. Yosemite National Park, in California, is famous for its granite arches and domes. The Needles, in the Black Hills of South Dakota, are towers of weathered granite.

SYENITE (pages 12 and 47) looks like granite, but contains little or no quartz. Feldspar is the most important mineral, though syenite may also contain amphibole, mica, and a few other things. Gray, pale yellow, and pink or grayish pink are the commonest colors. Syenite is found in the White Mountains of New England, in Montana, and in many other regions.

DIORITE (pages 12 and 47) is a dark member of the granitic group. It contains white feldspar and dark minerals such as amphiboles, pyroxene, and black mica. Some varieties of diorite contain no quartz, and others have very little. Most diorite is gray or grayish green.

Flow structure (page 47) was produced when doughy magma flowed slowly as it cooled and hardened. This made the different minerals collect in wavy or irregular bands that resemble bands in the made-over rock called gneiss. Flow structure shows most plainly in granite, syenite and diorite.

ANORTHOSITE (page 12) ranges from white to dull yellow, brown, or dark gray; some deposits resemble dark marble. The most important mineral in anorthosite is gray feldspar. Most deposits also contain tiny grains of pyroxene and magnetite. Another impurity makes the rock glow with a dark blue color. There are huge masses of anorthosite among the Adirondack Mountains of New York.

Syenite with Flow Structure

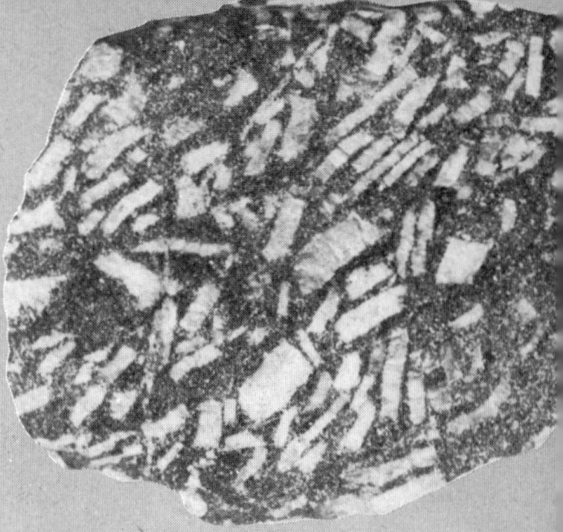

Syenite Porphyry

Graphic Granite

Diorite

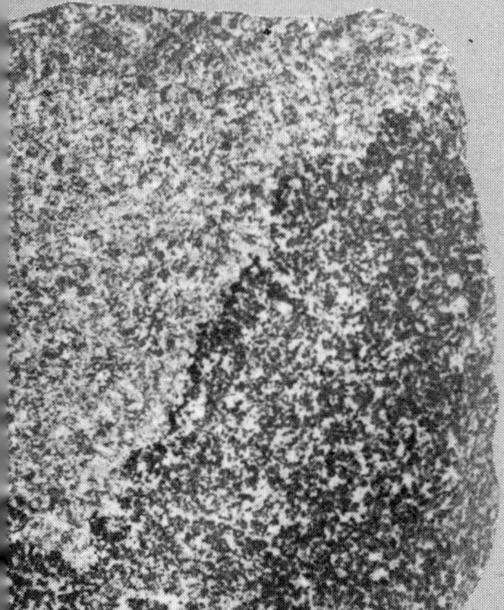

Diabase

Gabbro

GABBRO (page 47) is darker than diorite and most anorthosite, for it ranges from dark gray to black and blackish green. It contains feldspar as well as amphiboles and other dark minerals. The feldspar looks glassy or waxy and forms irregular grains or small blocks.

DIABASE (pages 47 and 88) is another dark rock. It contains feldspar, pyroxene and magnetite; flakes of mica and tiny pyrite crystals are common. Unlike granite, diabase is a rock that sometimes hardened underground and sometimes flowed out upon the surface. The Palisades of the Hudson, opposite New York City, are diabase that hardened underground. Thick flows, containing copper, are found in northern Michigan. Unfortunately, diabase varies so much that it is hard to identify. Like other so-called traprocks, it is tough and is often crushed for use in making concrete.

Have you ever heard miners talk about porphyry? Porphyry (page 47) is any igneous rock that contains large blocks or crystals of certain minerals. These generally are feldspar. They show that some minerals hardened faster than others, and so became much larger. The feldspar blocks in some deposits of granite are as much as two inches thick.

Sediment and Strata

Let's now examine three specimens that are very different from lava, and from rocks that belong to the granitic group. One piece consists of pebbles fastened together. Another specimen is made up of sand grains. The third is a mixture of pebbles, sand and mud, some of which is very fine.

These three specimens introduce us to rocks made of material that settled on land or in water. We call this material *sediment,* from a Latin word meaning "something that settles." Rocks made of sediment are said to be *sedimentary.*

A swift river that flows from hills or mountains shows us how sediment sometimes forms rocks. The river contains large boulders, as well as smaller pieces of stone that are being washed downstream. We watch mud and sand grains go by, while pebbles roll or skip along the bottom. Boulders move much more slowly, but now and then we hear them go *thud!* as they roll against each other.

On and on the river flows till it comes to a broad valley. There the rushing water slows down and loses most of its power to move things. As a result, its sediment settles, forming beds in which mud, sand, pebbles and large stones are jumbled together.

Next we examine a river that winds across almost level land. Here we find only mud, sand and small pebbles, for the water flows too slowly to roll large stones downstream. When the river overflows, however, it does spread layers of sediment over near-by lowlands. At other times mud and sand settle in bars which really are low, moist islands.

We find some of these islands as we follow the winding stream. We also discover that streams do not leave all their sediment in bars and upon lowlands. Much of it is rolled or carried along until it comes to the sea. There it is mixed with sediment which waves have worn from the coast.

If we watch a coast when waves roll in, we can see that the water is darkened by its load of sediment. In time, however, most of this load settles. Cobbles, pebbles, and coarse sand sink near shore or are piled up in beach deposits. Fine sand and coarse mud go out to sea, and fine mud is carried still farther. Sediment that has been dissolved goes farthest of all. It may not sink to the sea bottom until it is many miles from the shore.

This mixture of cobbles, pebbles and clay was deposited in the bed of an ancient stream.

Bars of sediment have settled in this sluggish river, which flows across almost level land.

Beds, or strata, of sedimentary rock. These form walls in the canyon of the Little Colorado River, in Arizona.

There are several ways to recognize rocks made of sediment. One way is to look for large stones, pebbles, sand, and mud grains. Agglomerate and tuff are the only igneous rocks made up of fragments fastened together. But bombs, cinders, and grains of volcanic ash will help you tell these deposits from others made of sediment.

A second way to tell sedimentary rocks is to look for remains of shells, corals, and other things that once were alive. These remains have often been mixed with sand, mud, and material that once was dissolved. In fact, dead things themselves become sediment and often form deposits of rock. Many limestones were made in this way, and so were several other rocks.

The third way to tell sedimentary rocks is to notice their layers. These layers were formed as material settled on land or in the water. In most places, layers of sediment settled one on top of another until they formed beds, or *strata*. Many strata are four or five inches thick, but those made of sand or pebbles may be ten to twenty feet in thickness.

You may find layers in deposits of volcanic ash that settled in lakes, but these are not very common. You may also find sheets of hardened lava that lie on top of each other or between beds of agglomerate. From a distance both may look like strata—but not when you come near them. They are irregular and contain the wrong kinds of rock; the lava shows bubbles, flow marks and columns, while agglomerate contains bombs, cinders, and other things made during eruptions. You will have no trouble telling such beds from the layers and strata in rocks made of sediment.

Conglomerate, Sandstone and Shale

We have said that rocks are large natural deposits of mineral material or coal. This means that beds of gravel, sand and clay are rocks. They are loose, or *unconsolidated,* sedimentary rocks, which have not been packed or cemented into stone.

Many unconsolidated rocks are being formed today. Others settled a long time ago, and some are very old. The unconsolidated deposit shown on page 50 settled in a wide valley more than sixty million years ago. During all that time it has remained a mixture of pebbles and clay, and has not become stone.

There also are many solid rocks made of sediment. Some consist of minerals that came from solution and hardened almost as soon as they settled. Other beds remained loose, or unconsolidated, for ages. In time, however, some of their minerals began to change while other minerals were deposited between their pieces or grains. In this way the loose stuff was cemented into beds of stone.

We'll skip the unconsolidated deposits, for most of them can be recognized without any difficulty. Instead of describing things we already know, let's examine some solid sedimentary rocks and find out how they were made.

CONGLOMERATE (page 54) is a rock whose name means "something mixed together." Most conglomerate is

Oil Shale

Pisolitic Bauxite

Catlinite,
or Pipestone

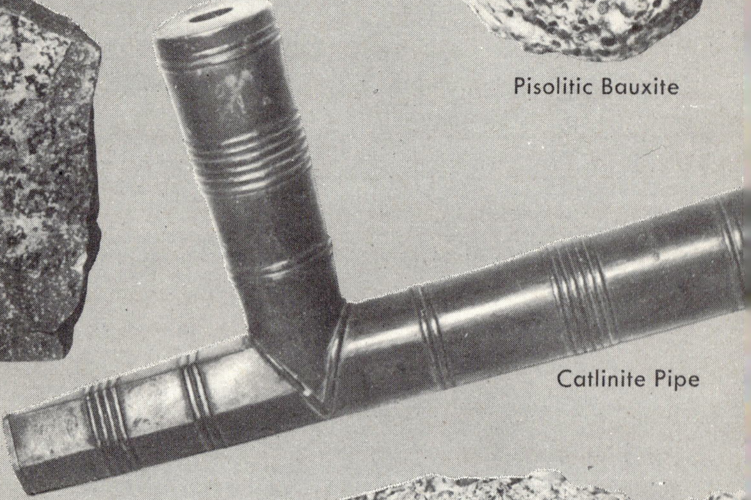

Catlinite Pipe

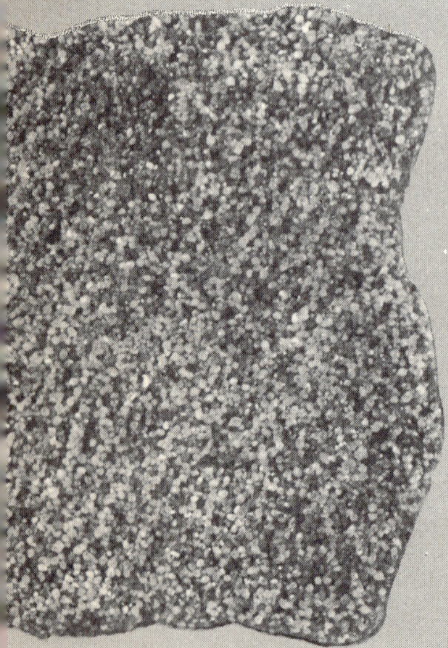

Coarse Sandstone

Conglomerate

a mixture of clay, sand, pebbles, and even boulders, fastened together by cement. Dark varieties look so much like Christmas plum pudding that we sometimes call them pudding stones.

Many beds of conglomerate in the West were formed at a time when mountains were being pushed upward. Swift streams washed sediment from the mountains and spread it out in valleys. At first there was a separate deposit for each stream, but in time the deposits became so wide that they overlapped. They also hardened into conglomerate that contains many large boulders and worn cobblestones.

Other beds of conglomerate contain nothing larger than pebbles. These beds are long and narrow, and seldom are very thick. They probably settled in river channels, just as long pebbly bars form in many rivers today.

The most widespread deposits of conglomerate settled in shallow water, near the shores of ancient seas. Long after the seas disappeared, the pebbly rock was pushed upward until it became land.

Hardened clay and various minerals cement the pebbles in conglomerate. Light-colored conglomerates may be cemented by calcite, clay or quartz. Brown deposits generally contain limonite. Although the mineral may be hard, it gives the rock a worn and rusty appearance.

SANDSTONE (page 54) is just what its name tells us. It is a rock made of sand grains cemented together. In some beds the cement is so weak that you can dig into the rock with a stick or crumble it between your fingers. Other sandstones are so firmly cemented that they are harder than glass. Quartzite is a very hard, changed form of sandstone which Indians often used for spearheads and knives.

"Pure" sandstone consists of quartz grains, but "impure" varieties contain feldspar, magnetite, and other minerals.

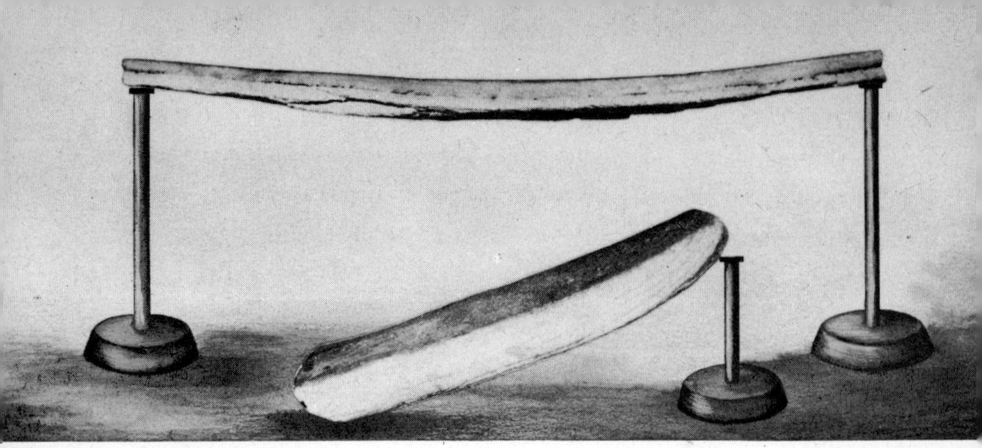

Two bent pieces of flexible sandstone.

White sandstone is cemented by quartz or calcite, but dark-colored deposits are held together by limonite, hematite, or hardened clay. Sandstone cemented by hematite and red clay forms bright-colored cliffs, especially in the West.

Flexible sandstone is light-colored, porous rock from which some material has been dissolved. This allows grains and layers to move or bend, though they do not fall apart. *Itacolumite* is flexible sandstone that contains flakes of mica. It is found in Brazil.

Arkose is coarse-grained sandstone that contains large amounts of feldspar in chips, lumps, and small blocks. Most arkose also contains large pebbles and so resembles conglomerate. You can tell it by its feldspar, however.

Greywacke, or *graywacke,* is brown, dark gray, or blackish sandstone that grades into conglomerate. It contains quartz, feldspar, dark minerals, and bits of dark rocks, all mixed together. It often makes up very thick beds.

Sandstones have formed in lakes, seas and rivers, as well as on land. It may be hard to tell where a special bed or deposit did settle unless it contains fossils. You may be sure that sandstone containing fossil sea shells was deposited in a sea or ocean. Tracks of land animals mean that the rock formed on land. Fresh-water shells and plants in a bed of sandstone tell us that the rock settled in a lake or stream.

SHALE is not so coarse as sandstone, for it is made of clay. Shale may be soft enough to be cut with a knife, or it may be hard. It generally consists of thin layers that can be split apart. Gray, buff, green, and red are the commonest colors. Most red shale contains hematite.

Oil shale (page 54) produces oil when it is heated; someday we shall get gasoline and fuel oil from it. *Bauxite* (page 54) is clay or shale that also is aluminum ore. Pure bauxite is white, but most deposits are colored yellow, brown, or red by impurities. Much bauxite is said to be pisolitic, because it contains balls that resemble small peas.

CATLINITE, or pipestone (page 54), is clay that has been changed into compact rock that is dark red or is mottled with pink. When freshly dug, it can be cut with a knife, but it becomes hard. Indians once used catlinite for peace pipes. The ancient quarries may be seen in the Pipestone National Monument, in southwestern Minnesota. There an Indian cuts and carves small souvenirs which he sells to visitors.

ARGILLITE (page 75) is a hard rock much like shale. Some argillite contains a great deal of quartz; some was hardened and changed when mountains were made. Colors range from gray and green to brown, red or purple. Mountains of changed argillite may be seen in Glacier National Park, Montana.

Like sandstones, shaly rocks formed in seas, lakes and rivers, and on lowlands that were flooded by streams. Most marine shales contain fossils of corals, "shellfish," and other sea-dwellers. Some red shales that settled on lowlands show footprints of dinosaurs.

Limestone and Dolomite

We find limestone in quarries, on hills, and in other places. Like all sedimentary rocks, it consists of layers and beds that lie one on top of another. Layers of limestone are thin, but beds may be several feet thick.

Most formations of limestone settled in ancient seas. Rivers that flowed into those seas brought limy material which had been dissolved from rocks on near-by lands. When this dissolved material reached salt water, it turned into particles of calcite. The particles then settled to the bottom, forming mud that became limestone.

We know that most limestone settled in seas because it contains remains of corals, oysters, starfish, and other sea-dwellers. Some limestones settled in lakes, however, and others were deposited in caves. One variety was made by hot springs. Their water dissolved calcite from rocks underground and brought it to the surface. There the calcite settled in beds of spongy-looking stone.

LIMESTONE (pages 59 and 61) is easy to recognize, in spite of its variations. It is a rock that consists mostly of calcite in grains, blocks, or other forms. Pure limestone is white or creamy and has a hardness of 3. The rock also bubbles when acid is dropped upon it, just as calcite does. Impure limestone may be harder than 3, but it can always be scratched by a knife. Impurities consist of clay, sand, limo-

Limestone

Tufa

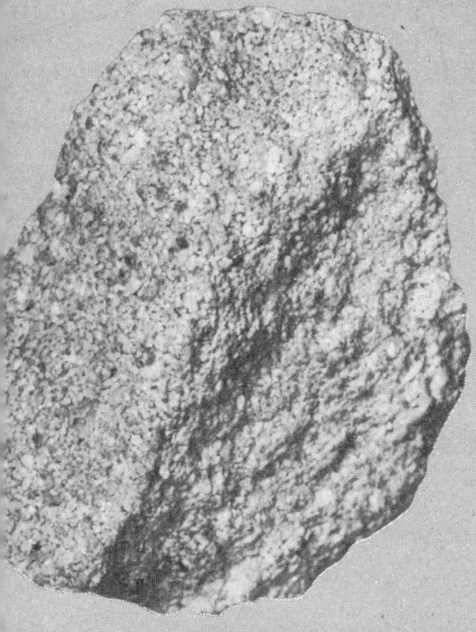
Shell Limestone

Chalk

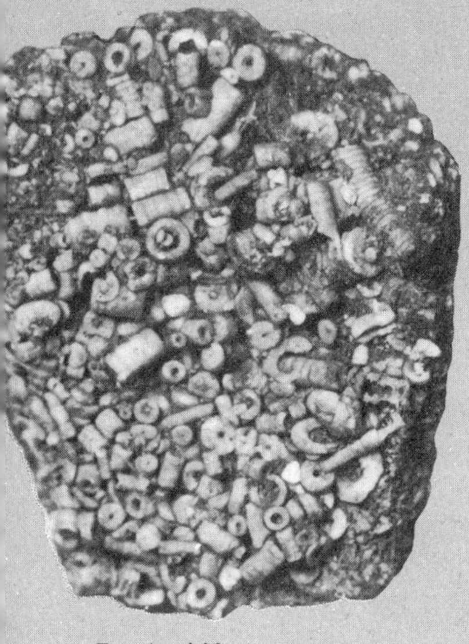
Encrinal Limestone

Coquina

nite, hematite, carbon, or other materials. They make the rock buff, brownish, red, gray, or even dull green. Beds that contain carbon are bluish gray or black.

Lithographic limestone is a very fine-grained variety; it also is so nearly pure that some beds are more than 98 per cent calcite. Lithographic limestone breaks with a shell-like fracture; trimmed specimens look very much like the chert shown on page 65. Smoothed slabs of lithographic limestone are used in printing fine maps and designs.

Limestone made up largely of dead remains may be named for them. Most *coral limestone,* for example, contains the remains of corals; they show plainly in polished or weathered slabs. *Encrinal limestone* (page 59) is full of broken plates and stems of creatures called crinoids, or "sea lilies." Although crinoids look like plants, they really are related to starfish.

Coquina (page 59) is made up of small shells. They are so poorly cemented that the rock crumbles easily. Since spaces between the shells are not filled by hardened mud, coquina is lightweight and porous. Deposits of this rock have formed along the eastern coast of Florida since the end of the Ice Age, ten to fifteen thousand years ago. Coquina also is found in other tropical and near-tropical regions.

Shell limestone (page 59) consists of broken and ground-up shells. It is not so porous as coquina, for its pieces are smaller. It is soft when it comes from the ground, but hardens as it dries. On Bermuda and some other southern islands, people saw freshly quarried shell limestone into blocks, dry them, and use them in building houses.

Chalk (page 59) is soft, crumbly limestone made of shells too small to be seen without a strong magnifying glass. Limestone made of calcite balls is *oolite* or *pisolite* (page 61). Oolite looks like fish eggs, but the balls in pisolite are

Dolomite

"Coral Rock" of Florida

Oolite

Travertine

Onyx

Pisolite

A block of dolomite formed by simple plants that lived on the bottom of an ancient sea.

larger. The names of these two varieties mean "eggstone" and "peastone."

Some oolite consists of grains that were piled upon seashores by wind, but pisolite settled in water. In Indiana, thickly bedded oolite is quarried for building stone. Known as Indiana limestone, it is light gray to buff in color. Almost every city in the United States has buildings that are made of Indiana limestone, or are trimmed with it. Can you find one of these buildings near your home?

Tufa (page 59) is rather brittle and spongy, or porous. It forms in many hot springs, under waterfalls, and on the shores of desert lakes. There are beautiful tufa deposits at Mammoth Hot Springs, in Yellowstone National Park. Curio stores sometimes sell imitation birds' nests made of sticks, with clay eggs, all covered with white tufa.

Travertine (page 61) is harder and more compact than tufa. Much travertine is tufa deposits of ancient hot springs, made harder and more compact by water seeping through the ground. Many "cave formations" are travertine deposited by water seeping or trickling into caves. First the water dissolves calcite from beds of limestone. Then it deposits the calcite again in forms that look like curtains, towers, and stony icicles. Some of these things have been forming for many millions of years.

Beds of travertine are often sawed into slabs and polished for use in floors and the inside walls of large buildings. If you see a wall covered with slabs of whitish or buff limestone containing flattened, irregular holes, you may be sure the rock is travertine.

Onyx (page 61) also is a cave deposit, but it is crystalline. The finest onyx consists of crumpled, irregular layers that are stained different colors by impurities. This colored rock is cut and polished for use in inkstands, lamp bases, vases, and other ornaments.

DOLOMITE (page 61) looks like limestone, but does not bubble when acid is dropped on it. This means that more than half the rock consists of the mineral also called dolomite. The rock never is so fine-grained as lithographic limestone, nor so crumbly as chalk. It also never takes the form of coquina, though it may contain shells. Some ancient dolomite resembles the rock called "coral rock" in southern Florida. Other dolomite was made by simple plants which grew upon sea bottoms and were covered with mineral grains. In this way the plants built up beds of stone while they were still alive.

Rocks Made of Quartz

Indians of ancient times had no steel and very little copper. When they wanted a knife, spearhead, arrow point, or ax they had to make it from stone. They also made stone dishes in which to cook their food.

Different kinds of rock were used for different purposes. Basalt, for example, made good food grinders, and obsidian was fine for spearheads, knives, and sharp scrapers. In many places, however, obsidian could not be found. There the Indians often made their weapons from rocks consisting of fine-grained quartz.

CHERT (page 65) is the commonest of these fine-grained quartz rocks, and the one most often used in spears, arrowheads and knives. Chert is about as hard as crystals of quartz. It breaks with a shell-like, or conchoidal, fracture that produces sharp edges and points. It often looks waxy or greasy, but sometimes resembles broken china. Though some chert is white, impurities generally color it gray, black, yellow, brown or iron red.

In some places chert forms layers and beds, but it often consists of irregular lumps and nodules that lie in beds of limestone. Some nodules formed while the lime mud was settling, but others were made when water dissolved particles of calcite and left quartz particles in their place. Chert often forms pebbles when limestone is worn away.

Flint Nodule from Chalk

Chert

Flint, showing Patina

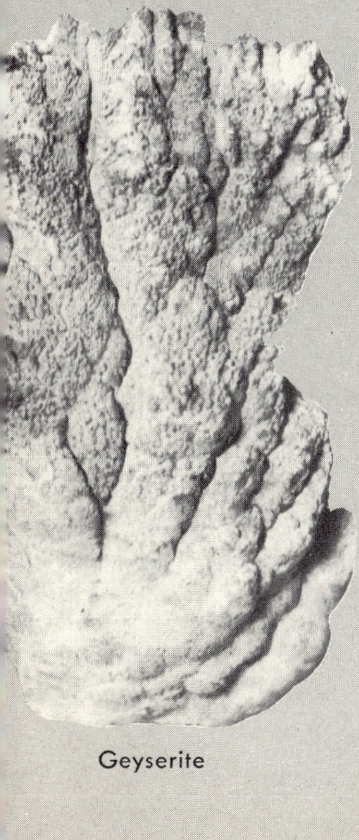

Geyserite

Chert Nodules
in Limestone

Jasper is a red or reddish-brown variety of chert which often contains large quartz grains. *Jaspillite* is much like jasper, but contains layers of hematite; it is found in iron mines near Lake Superior. *Jasperoid* is a dark gray or brownish variety of chert found in southwestern Missouri and near-by regions. It fills the spaces between broken bits of pale gray chert. This broken and cemented rock, called breccia, is shown on page 92.

FLINT (page 65) is not so common as chert, especially in the United States. It is made up of very fine-grained quartz and impurities which generally color it brown, dark gray or black. It is both more brittle and finer grained than chert, and breaks with a better conchoidal fracture. The edges of thin chips are yellowish or translucent, which means that light comes through them.

Like chert, flint forms layers as well as nodules. When it is weathered, it first becomes smooth and bright. Then it turns into a dull, powdery-looking crust called *patina*. Many ancient stone implements show crusts of patina. The finest nodules of dark-colored flint are found in the chalk beds of England and France.

GEYSERITE (page 65) is another rock made of quartz, but it does not look like flint or chert. It is a white, brittle deposit built by geysers and some hot springs. Hot water dissolves quartz deep down underground and brings it to the surface. There the quartz settles in layers or spongy-looking masses which often resemble biscuits or cauliflowers. They can easily be told from travertine because they do not bubble when acid is dropped on them. The finest deposits of geyserite are found in Yellowstone National Park and near-by parts of Wyoming.

Coal from Ancient Plants

Rattle-clatter-bang! Lumps of coal are being unloaded from a truck. Down the chute and into a basement they go, but the truckman throws out a piece of gray shale. "Here's something," he may say, "for your rock collection!"

The shale will not burn, and it is not coal. Still, dark markings on its surface tell us how coal was made. Long ago, during a part of earth history called the Coal Age, the marks were trees, ferns, and rushes that grew in a swamp. The trees and ferns lived on low, moist ground. Most of the rushes, however, stood in shallow, muddy water.

When these plants in the ancient swamp died, they fell into the water. There they lay and decayed very slowly while mud settled upon them. The decayed plants became black marks, or films, of carbon while the mud hardened into shale.

At last a time came when water in the swamp grew clear—so clear that it had no mud to settle upon the bottom. But plants kept right on dying and falling into the water. In time, they formed beds of dark, spongy material called muck. It was much like peat, which is forming today in many bogs and swamps.

Year after year the muck became thicker, until it began to turn into coal. Meanwhile, the country was changing. Low places were pushed up into hills, and the swamp became

Plant remains in this shale tell how coal was made.

moist land. Swift rivers ran from the hills and wound among the forests. After heavy rains, the rivers overflowed. When they did so, they covered the ground with muddy sand that hardened into sandstone. Often the sand beds buried tree trunks and killed them. We may see fossils of these trees in some cliffs of Coal Age rock.

All coal has been made from dead, decayed plants, but not all coal formed in the Coal Age. This part of earth history is also known as the Carboniferous (carbon-bearing), or Pennsylvanian, Age. It began more than 250 million years ago. It lasted many millions of years, while coal beds formed in swamps that extended from Texas to the northern Atlantic Coast.

At last the Coal Age came to an end. Three long ages went by before swamps again became so big that muck could settle in them and turn into beds of coal. Those new swamps were in the West. The reptiles called dinosaurs waded in them, leaving footprints in layers of sand or mud between the beds of coal.

Coal also settled in swamps of the West long after the Era of Reptiles ended. This coal is not so hard or so dark as the coal that formed during earlier times, but it forms very thick beds.

Last of all came the swamps and bogs in which peat has formed. Most of these swamps and bogs began at the end of the Ice Age, after the last great glaciers melted. Few peat deposits are more than ten thousand years old, and many are much less. In fact, peat still is forming as dead mosses and other plants accumulate in lakes and bogs.

Actually, several different kinds of rock are made of decayed plant material. We generally arrange them in the *coal series,* beginning with the one that is youngest and least like black, brittle stone:

PEAT (page 70) is a soft, spongy deposit made of plants that have not fully decayed. It generally is yellowish or dull brown, and is coarse as well as very soft. This variety of peat is often sold in bales, to be mixed with soil in lawns or gardens. A black variety is much finer, and looks like clay when it is wet. Black peat probably resembles coal muck. It has lain at the bottom of bogs so long that the fibers of moss, grass, and other plants have almost disappeared.

LIGNITE, or BROWN COAL (page 70), is finer and more compact than peat, though it is not solid. Lignite is yellow brown or dull black; it often contains bits of wood and tough stems. When dry, it burns very quickly. It may also catch fire without being lighted, by the process called spontaneous combustion. Great care must be used in storing lignite in buildings or coalbins.

Four rocks that belong to the coal series. They are made up of plant material rather than minerals, which merely form impurities and so are unimportant.

SUBBITUMINOUS COAL is also called SEMIBITUMINOUS. It is finer, darker, and a little harder than lignite, though the two look alike in pictures. Subbituminous coal burns easily and is a good fuel for stoves, furnaces, and steam engines. Beds of this coal in the state of Montana are twenty to thirty feet thick, and are mined with huge electric shovels. One shovel will dig a carload of coal in about six minutes.

BITUMINOUS, or SOFT, COAL (page 70) is a brittle rock that generally is deep black. It is made up of dull and shiny layers. The shiny material was formed from decayed tree trunks and branches, but dull layers were made of leaves and small bits of plant material. Bituminous coal generally breaks into large, sharp-edged blocks, though its hardness is only 1 to 2.

ANTHRACITE, or HARD COAL (page 70), is a dense, brittle rock with a steely or jet-black color and a glassy or metallic surface. Its hardness is 2 or more. Most anthracite once was soft coal, but was squeezed and changed when parts of the earth were crumpled into mountains. This got rid of most of the material that makes sooty smoke when soft, or bituminous, coal is burned. A great deal of anthracite is mined from ancient, worn-down mountains in the state of Pennsylvania.

Roots of a Coal-age tree are preserved in this block of shale from a cliff at Joggins, Nova Scotia.

Marks in Beds of Stone

Suppose we watch a muddy pond during a long dry season. Day by day the water evaporates, becoming lower and lower until it disappears. When that happens the mud dries out and begins to crack. Soon the cracks form a criss-crossed network. It divides the mud into sections that have several sides and so are known as polygons.

Many rocks contain mud-cracked layers that formed during ancient times (page 75). They began when mud dried out and cracked, just as it does today. Month after month it baked in the sun, until it became hard. At last water covered it again, bringing more sediment. It covered the dry polygons and filled the cracks between them. In this way the mud cracks were preserved while the layers slowly turned into stone.

Ancient mud cracks are commonest in shale, but we may also find them in limestone, argillite, and shaly sandstone. Some of the cracked beds settled in lakes or in ponds that were made by rivers when they overflowed. Other beds formed in seas so shallow that water often disappeared from shoals and long bays. Most mud-cracked limestones formed in such seas. So did many shales and sandstones.

Beds that contain ancient mud cracks may also show *ripple marks* (page 76). These marks look like rippling ridges on strata or layers of stone.

A slab of sandstone will show us how most ripple marks formed. The stone, of course, began as sand that settled in shallow water. Breezes blew over the surface, stirring the water into waves. As the waves reached the bottom they moved grains of sand and piled them into ridges. Between these ridges the waves left furrows with gently rounded bottoms.

We call such ripple marks *symmetrical* because they slope equally on both sides. Symmetrical marks are always made by waves. Big waves produce big marks—some of those in beds of limestone are as much as seven feet high. Small waves make much smaller marks, for those in some strata measure less than an inch from ridge to ridge.

Many slabs of sandstone are covered with *interference ripples.* They show that the wind suddenly changed and sent waves in a new direction. Because of this, they built new ridges across the old ones. Low places between inter-

Mud cracks in a pond that is drying up, or evaporating.

ference ripples are sometimes called "tadpole nests," although they are not fossils.

Current ripples are made either by wind or by water. Their ridges are not symmetrical, for each one has a steep side and a side that slopes gently. This shows that a current pushed sediment up the gentle slope and then let it roll down the steep one. The gentle slope is always the one up which the current and sediment moved.

Many current ripples now form in rivers, as they did during ancient times. Other ripples are piled up by currents that flow along shores, or by winds that blow steadily in one direction. These wind-made ripples generally are smaller than those made by water. They also are much less common in ancient rocks.

Ripple marks of all sorts are most common in sandstone, for grains of sand roll about very easily. Current ripples are rare in other rocks, but interference marks are sometimes found in beds of sandy shale. Symmetrical ripple marks are found in shale, too, and even in beds of limestone. Some of these marks are so large that they must have been made by big waves that rolled across the sea. Other ripple marks in limestone are very small. We wonder how little waves could pile such sticky stuff as lime mud into symmetrical ridges.

In collecting ripple marks we must watch out for "negatives." These are beds or layers that covered ripple marks and filled the furrows between them. This makes them just the opposite of true ripple marks. When such "negatives" break up into slabs, they show ridges that are wide and rounded, and furrows that are narrow and sharp. You must turn such slabs right side up to see how they once fitted over ripple-marked beds.

Rain prints (page 77) are sometimes found on beds of shaly sandstone. The prints were made by raindrops that

Mud cracks in a slab of limestone. The cracks also are filled with limy material that has hardened into stone.

Coarse, wide mud cracks in shaly sandstone.

The slab at the right shows the under side of a slab of mud-cracked argillite in Glacier National Park, Montana.

Interference ripple marks, made when waves changed direction.

A negative of interference rippl marks.

Ripple marks made by current (left) always have one steep side

Symmetrical ripple marks (be low) have equal sides. They wer made by waves, most of whic were small.

"Fossil" salt crystals.

Rain prints in dried mud.

fell while the rock was soft. Each drop made a little saucer-shaped mark that remained when the deposit hardened.

Modern rain prints often make excellent specimens. Find some fine-grained, stiff mud and watch for a shower in which large drops fall very hard. When the shower ends, you may lift up a piece of mud that shows the finest rain prints. Lift the mud carefully, let it dry slowly, and then keep it on cotton or crumpled tissue paper in a cardboard box. If you don't drop it, such a specimen will last for years.

Some layers of sandstone are covered with things that look like little blocks or boxes. They once were crystals of salt that formed when beds of salty sea sand dried out. In time the salt disappeared, but grains of mud and sand took its place. These grains built up "fossil" *salt crystals* which were preserved when the sand hardened into stone.

Good specimens of "fossil" salt crystals are scarce. If you find some, collect them carefully and keep them to exchange for other minerals or rocks.

What Cross Bedding Tells

Do you want a rock specimen made by winds that blew across an ancient desert? Would you like a record of streamlets that wandered over slopes no one ever saw? Do you need strata telling of waves or currents that shifted one way or another, millions of years ago?

You may have all these things if you look beside cliffs of *cross-bedded* sandstone. Take the cliff shown on the next page, for example. It was worn by rain and a stream that flows a short distance away. But the rock itself was made by winds—winds that blew across a desert and piled sand grains into hills called dunes. As the winds shifted to and fro, they piled layers of sand in different directions. Since the layers seem to cut across each other, they are said to be cross-bedded.

Cross bedding caused by shifting streams seldom shows so plainly. Sand that settles in streams is often mixed with mud and pebbles. When this mixture hardens, it forms coarse, dark sandstone in which the "crossed" layers may be very irregular. More regular cross bedding is produced where rivers build deltas as they flow into lakes or seas. Cross-bedded delta deposits cover many square miles.

When waves and currents pile up ripple marks, they produce cross bedding so thin that we call it *cross lamination.* Many layers in fine, cross-laminated sandstone are not much

A cliff of cross-bedded sandstone in southern Utah.

thicker than paper. They show plainly in specimens small enough to be kept in your collection.

Cross-bedded limestone is not common, but it can be found. Some deposits consist of oolite balls, but others are made of grains from worn, broken sea shells. This material really was sand—sand made of calcite, not quartz. Winds blew the calcite sand about and piled it into cross-bedded dunes. These then were cemented into limestone. The shell limestone shown on page 59 comes from dune deposits in the Bermuda Islands.

Concretions and Geodes

Many banks and hillsides contain things that look like balls, watches, or flattened cucumbers. Some even seem to have eyes. Others resemble stony turtles with round shells, heads and legs.

These oddly shaped stones are not petrified animals, but are *concretions* (page 81). They were made by water that soaked, or seeped, through beds of rock. As the water went along it dissolved mineral matter, such as iron compounds or calcite. Then it deposited the mineral matter again. As it did so, it fastened grains of sand, clay, or even calcite together and so built up concretions.

Many concretions developed around roots; they are long and slender, or are shaped like rings. Other concretions were formed around leaves, such as those of ferns that lived and died during the Coal Age, and were buried in beds of shale. Such concretions generally are oval or look like flattened cucumbers. When we break them open with a chisel, we find prints of the ancient leaves.

Other concretions "grew" around clay particles, or around small lumps of mineral matter. Some of these concretions are round and flat, or are shaped like balls. Others resemble turtles, toads, or strings of beads. Some have such elaborate shapes that they look as if they had been made by hand, like fine jewelry.

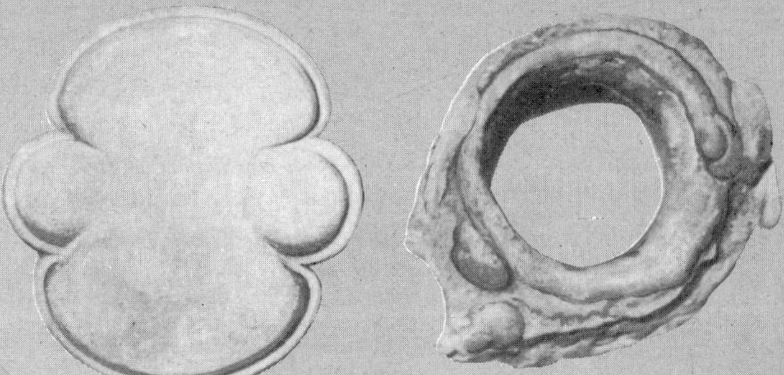

Flat and Ring-shaped Concretions

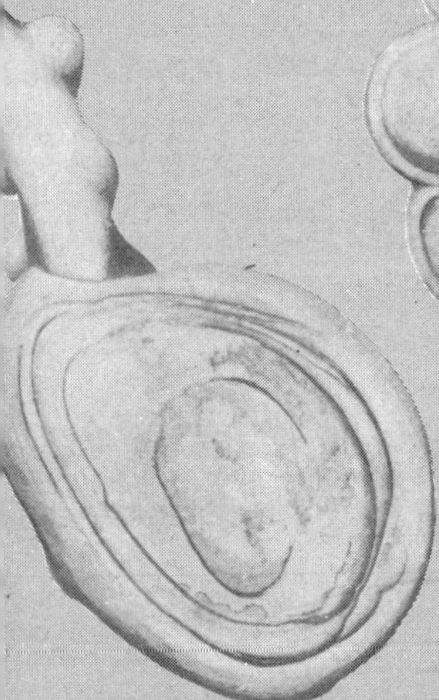

Claystone Concretion

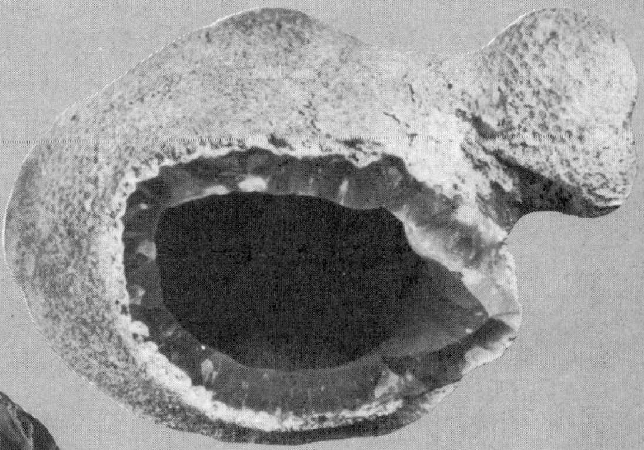

Geode in Coral

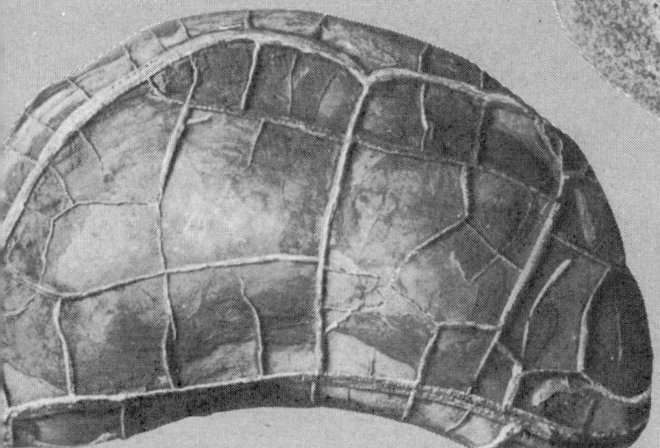

Septarian Concretion

Paintstone Concretion

Quartz Geode

We sometimes divide concretions into claystones and ironstones. Claystones are made of clay cemented by lime, or calcite. Ironstones consist of clay or sand cemented by rusty-looking limonite. But we have no special name for concretions of sand cemented by calcite, or for concretions found in limestone.

Paintstones (page 81) are ironstone concretions with soft, earthy centers. This earthy material generally is a mixture of limonite and clay, known as yellow ocher. Indians once mixed yellow ocher with grease, to make paint.

Rattlestones are hollow concretions containing pebbles that rattle when they are shaken. Most rattlestones consist of sand cemented by hard limonite. When they are broken they look a good deal like the shells of coconuts.

Septaria (page 81) are often called petrified turtles. They really are concretions that were cracked while they lay in the ground. Water filled the cracks with mineral grains or crystals. Since the fillings generally are thicker than the concretions, they form a network of ridges. Sometimes the fillings remain while the concretions crumble away. Such septaria look like bits of gigantic honeycomb.

Many concretions are small—so small you can put several of them into one pocket. Others are very large, and weigh hundreds or even thousands of pounds. When rain washes the soft rock away from these big concretions, they look like cannon balls, petrified logs, or enormous mushrooms of stone. Toadstool Park, in the northwestern part of Nebraska, is a place where huge, irregular concretions stand out on ridges and stems because the rock around them has been worn away. In general, the largest concretions are found in sandstone, while the smallest ones come from fine-grained clay.

When *geodes* (page 81) come out of the ground, they

look very much like rough concretions. Actually, they are holes partly filled with minerals. When geodes are neatly broken in half, we can see this mineral filling and the empty space inside it.

Sometimes the seeping water that made geodes left quartz in thin layers of agate or chalcedony. More often, the tiny particles of mineral matter were built into crystals with smooth sides, straight edges, and sharp points. Most of these crystals also are quartz, but some geodes contain calcite and other minerals.

Perhaps the strangest geodes of all are found on the Florida coast, near the city of Tampa. There water seeping through beds of limestone has dissolved the centers of fossil corals. Then more water lined the holes with chalcedony, the variety of quartz that never forms crystals but has a waxy appearance. The chalcedony in most of these geodes is brownish, purplish, or dark, dull blue.

If you visit western Florida, be sure to look for fossil corals that have been worn from beds of limestone. If you find one that is light in weight, take it home and break it open carefully. It will probably be a coral geode, and a fine specimen for your rock collection.

Veins and Dikes

"Lucky stones" are dark-colored pebbles with white or pale pink stripes. There may be just one stripe to a pebble, going all the way through it and coming to its surface all the way round. There also may be several stripes that run in different directions or even go crisscross.

The stripes on most lucky stones are *veins*. Those shown on page 85 began while the pebble still was part of a stone ledge. Although the ledge seemed to be solid, it really contained many cracks. Water soaked through the cracks, leaving calcite or quartz. When these minerals filled the cracks, the fillings became veins. Later, when the ledge broke to pieces, parts of two crossed veins were in the piece that became this pebble, or lucky stone.

There really are three kinds of veins, formed in three different ways. The kind we have described was made by ordinary water that worked into the ground. There it dissolved quartz and calcite, and carried them along as it went. Then when the water came to cracks, it left the minerals in them. Bit by bit the mineral grains built up light-colored veins.

The second kind of vein was made by hot water, often in the form of steam. This water came from very hot rock or magma, deep down underground. Instead of sinking, the water worked its way upward till it came to cracks in rocks

(*Left*) Veins of rock that once was molten. It now resembles light-colored granite surrounded by dark stone. (*Right*) This "lucky stone" contains veins of calcite deposited by water that seeped through the ground.

near the surface. There the water cooled and left minerals which it had brought from the hot rocks far below. Sometimes those minerals formed veins of ore. People now mine such veins for gold, silver, and other valuable metals.

Veins of the third kind were made by molten material that squeezed into cracks near the earth's surface. When the molten material hardened it became basalt, diabase, or some other igneous rock. Most of these veins that once were molten are too thick to be seen in pebbles such as lucky stones.

Suppose we now ask a riddle: when is a vein not a vein? The answer is, when it measures more than six or eight inches in thickness. Thick veins are known as *dikes*, a name that is also spelled *dykes*.

No true dikes were made by water that soaked down from

This weathered dolomite contains veins of quartz deposited by hot water or steam that came from hot or even molten rocks far below the earth's surface.

the surface. Some have been made by hot water from magma, especially when the magma was granite. The rest once were molten rock, like the third kind of vein.

When the land is worn down, or eroded, big dikes often stand out much higher than the rocks around them. From a distance they look like walls built by human beings. For this reason, dikes often are given names such as Great Wall, Chinese Wall (after a huge man-made wall in northern China), and Giant's Wall.

Crusts and Imitation Plants

The dark gray specimen shown on page 88 came from a boulder of diabase. The boulder was covered with a yellowish crust. It still shows on two sides of the specimen.

The yellowish crust is not something that formed when the diabase hardened. The crust also is not a vein, for veins never form *around* rocks. The yellowish material was produced after a ledge of diabase had broken into boulders. Rain water soaked into them and changed their minerals. Some of the minerals became porous or crumbly. Others that contained iron turned into limonite. In this way they made the yellowish crust, which looks rusty and is more crumbly than the diabase that has not been changed.

You may find weathered crusts on many pebbles and boulders. In dry regions, you may also find rocks covered with crusts that resemble tufa. They consist of calcite dissolved by rain water that soaked into the ground. Then the water came back to the surface and evaporated. As it did so, it left crusts of calcite on ledges, boulders, and small stones. Many crusts, of course, are still being formed.

Dendrites (page 88) resemble small, stony plants. By using our imaginations, we can see their stems and leaves.

Dendrites are not plants, however, in spite of their appearance. They also are not clusters of crystals, like the fern-shaped clusters of frost crystals that often form on window-

Dendrites

Dark-colored Diabase
with a Weathered Crust

Moss Agate

panes. Instead, the markings consist of mineral grains left by water seeping through the ground. In some specimens the mineral is pyrite, but it generally is a manganese compound. Manganese, as you know, is a metal used to make steel hard and tough.

Dendrites sometimes are covered by layers of quartz. When the quartz is clear or pale and milky, this combination produces *moss* or *tree* agates. Most of the moss agates found among pebbles have indistinct markings, but very fine ones come from India. They usually are too expensive to be bought for rock collections.

Crumpled and Broken Rocks

Have you ever found a boulder made of layers that are crumpled like sheets of wastepaper? Such boulders tell one of the most surprising stories you will ever find in a stone.

Ages ago the layers were mud that settled in a sea. Sometimes the mud was dark and made dark-colored layers. At other times the mud was light colored, forming pale gray layers. Both kept their different colors when the mud turned into shale.

Millions of years went by—more years than we can imagine. Sometimes the bottom of the ancient sea was pushed upward until it became dry land. Sometimes the land sank until seas covered it again. Limestone, sandstone, and other rocks settled in the salty water or along the shore. These rocks, which became very thick, covered the hardened shale.

At last something new happened. Instead of going up or down, part of the earth began to push sidewise. Year after year it kept on pushing, with enormous force. It pushed against the beds of shale, limestone, and sandstone until they bent and then crumpled into great up-and-down folds. The downward folds became valleys. The upward folds were pushed so high that they formed mountain ranges.

Our boulder (page 90) was part of one of those ranges. The mountain itself has been worn away, but we can easily

This rock once contained layers of shale. The layers were squeezed, crumpled and changed as a range of mountains was built in what now is the state of Wyoming.

see wrinkles that developed when the shale was squeezed and folded. We also see crinkly bands of light-colored minerals such as quartz and feldspar. These were forced between the dark layers while they were being crumpled.

What would have happened if pressure had broken these layers of rock instead of crumpling them?

The upper specimen shown on page 91 answers this question. It came from a place where rocks were pushed and squeezed toward the left. Since the layers were hard and brittle, they broke. You can see several sharp breaks, as well as a band where the layers were shattered into chips.

The lower specimen is a piece of sandstone with dark and light layers. This rock was not squeezed and forced sideways, but was broken when the land moved upward or

Layers bent and broken by squeezing

Layers broken as land moved upward or downward

Jasperoid Breccia

Marble Breccia

downward. You can see how it broke into wedge-shaped pieces that also went up or down.

The breaks in these two specimens are called *faults.* Some faults are only a few inches high. Others are thousands of feet in height and run through the country for many miles. A fault east of the Sierra Nevada mountains in California is four hundred miles long. Rocks on one side of this break are at least fifteen thousand feet higher than those on the other side. Another fault in Montana and the Canadian province of Alberta was made when land was pushed upward and sideways. Rocks above the break were forced northeastward for twenty to thirty miles!

The only way to "collect" such great faults as these is to photograph them, or clip pictures from newspapers and magazines. However, we can often find pebbles containing crumpled layers or tiny faults. Both show best when the layers differ in color or in hardness.

BRECCIA is a rock made of sharp-edged, broken pieces cemented together into new beds. The commonest kind of breccia was made underground as rocks heaved upward or sank. The broken pieces show plainly, especially when they are fastened together by stone of a different color.

Made-over, or Metamorphic, Rocks

When we described the granitic group we found that old rocks can be made over into new ones. This process is called *metamorphism,* from an ancient Greek word that means "to change form." Rocks that have been made over are known as *metamorphic.*

Many rocks have been metamorphosed by heat and steam. Heat changes some of their minerals, while steam makes others combine with materials from the magma. Steam also dissolves minerals and leaves others in their place. All this turns the original rocks into new ones which may be quite different.

Folding and mountain-building also cause metamorphism. Folding bends rocks and squeezes them under tremendous pressure. Helped by heat and water deep down in the ground, it also changes minerals. Calcite and dolomite are turned into little crystalline blocks that may show plainly when the rock is polished or weathered. Some other minerals become flakes which are smooth and shiny.

These flakes generally are not scattered about any which way, like the flakes of mica in granite. Instead, they are arranged in sheets known as *folia.* Folia may be very much crumpled, but they generally can be split apart quite easily. Their shiny flakes, and the way they cut across bedding, show that they are not thin layers of sediment.

Metamorphism does one very strange thing: it often makes rocks which once were different look very much alike. Suppose granite, conglomerate, and coarse sandstone are changed, or metamorphosed. If the process goes on long enough, they become a new kind of rock called gneiss. In the same way, mountain-building has turned clay, shale, impure sandstone, dolomite, and even volcanic ash into another rock with thin folia. What counts here is the kind and effects of metamorphism, not the original rock.

GNEISS (page 95) has just been mentioned; it is a coarse-grained rock with rather poor folia. Gneiss contains quartz, feldspar, mica, and other minerals, and it seldom splits into sheets. Most granite gneiss has not been changed very much, and still looks like granite. Gneiss made from shale generally is dark, and has better folia than other types. Sandstone gneiss is so tough and strong that Indians often made axes from it.

SLATE is another metamorphic rock that has not been greatly changed. It once was gray, black, green or red shale, and it still has those colors. Metamorphism has changed some of the minerals, however, and has turned them into

Cleavage in this block of slate cuts across the layers that formed when the rock was mud that settled in an ancient sea.

Quartzite

Gneiss Formed from Sedimentary Rock

Granite Gneiss

Phyllite

Mica Schist

flakes. These are arranged in thin, flat sheets which split easily. This splitting is called *slaty cleavage*. It generally cuts across the original layers, which can be told only by their colors. Folded beds of slate may be seen in some cliffs and in the walls of large quarries.

SCHIST (pages 95 and 97) is the metamorphic rock made from clay, shale, sandstone, dolomite, lava or volcanic ash. Schist has been squeezed much harder than slate, and often has been crumpled into tighter folds. Its minerals also have been greatly changed. So many have been turned into flakes that schist splits easily into thin, crumpled folia that shine or are satiny in appearance. *Mica schist* (page 95) is the commonest variety; it contains large amounts of mica and splits easily. *Talc schist* (page 97) contains a great deal of talc. Most of the talc in talcum powder comes from this variety of schist.

PHYLLITE (page 95) is about halfway between slate and schist. Phyllite generally is dull red, yellow or greenish gray, and is much more brittle than slate. Its layers commonly are crumpled, and it feels rather greasy. The layers often contain small crystals of pyrite or garnet. Though some phyllite deposits began as shale, others once were lava or beds of volcanic tuff.

SOAPSTONE (page 97) is a dark gray or greenish rock made up of talc mixed with a few other minerals. Soapstone does not split into folia. Broken surfaces are rough, yet look silvery or satiny, and feel greasy. The rock can be sawed into slabs that are used for steps, washtubs, sinks and tables in chemical laboratories.

QUARTZITE (page 95) is a very hard, tough rock that still has its original beds. It was formed when water or steam deposited quartz around the grains of sand in sandstone. This built up tiny, irregular crystals that stick to each other

Fine-grained Marble

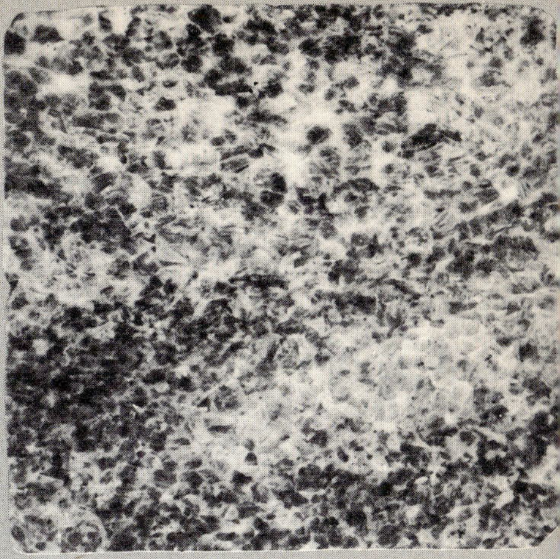

Coarse-grained Marble

Serpentine Bowl

Talc Schist

Soapstone

Serpentine

very tightly. Some layers and beds of quartzite are white. Others are colored pink, pale green or pale brown by clay and other impurities. Some beds of quartzite contain thin layers of mica that formed while the rock was being folded and squeezed. These layers allow the quartzite to split into large, satiny slabs.

MARBLE (page 97) is metamorphosed limestone or dolomite. Its minerals have been turned into crystalline blocks which may be as small as grains of sugar or as much as a half inch thick. You can tell whether these blocks are dolomite or calcite by putting acid on them. Acid will make calcite fizz, but will not make dolomite do so.

Pure marble is white, but most marble is not pure. It was made from rock that contained clay or other impurities. These impurities collected in cloudy, irregular bands which show how the rocks were squeezed and crumpled. Sometimes marble was broken as well as changed, forming breccia (page 92).

The name marble also is used for rock made of calcite that has been turned into small crystalline grains, although the beds have not been crumpled. This sort of marble often is gray, pink or brownish in color and contains well-preserved fossils. They make interesting patterns when slabs of the rock are polished.

SERPENTINE (page 97) is often called "verde antique" or "antique marble." It is made up of the mineral serpentine with quartz, calcite, dolomite or other materials. The most familiar variety of serpentine is very dark green and contains streaks of whitish calcite. Polished slabs of this rock are often used to decorate the inside walls of banks, railway stations, and other important buildings. You can easily see that calcite fills veins and spaces between the blocks of broken green serpentine.

A Scratched Stone's Story

A boulder lies in a valley among the mountains. Its curved face has many deep scratches that look as if they were made by a knife. Actually, the scratches tell us how the boulder got its shape. They also tell us what brought it to the valley, and why it lies among deposits of broken, worn stones and clay.

Boulders may be made of any kind of hard rock—basalt, granite, sandstone, and so on. This one consists of shaly limestone. We can see the different-colored layers on the boulder's curved, scratched face.

The limestone, we know, began as mud that settled in an ancient sea. Ages passed, and the old sea rocks were pushed upward. Up they went again and again. At last they formed mountains thousands of feet in height.

As the mountains became higher and higher, the weather around them changed. Cold winds howled over their ridges and peaks. Storms brought sleet and snow, even in the summertime. Snow piled into drifts so thick that sunshine could not melt them. When the drifts overlapped each other, they turned into snow fields.

The cold, white snow fields grew larger and larger—but they changed in another way, too. The snow packed together and froze into ice, so that snow fields became ice fields. Then the ice began to move, forming glaciers.

This boulder shows scratches, or striations, made while it was in a glacier. The deposit around the boulder is till.

One glacier appeared above the valley in which the scratched boulder now lies. At first the glacier was not very large, but it grew after every snowstorm. In time it spread down a steep slope and into the valley, filling it with ice that was more than a thousand feet in thickness.

As ice in the glacier moved, it pressed against the sides of the valley and squeezed into crevices. There it pushed, pried and pulled so hard that it broke off blocks of stone and carried them away. Other stones fell from cliffs and tumbled onto the glacier. Those that rolled into open cracks were covered by the moving ice.

The scratched boulder was one of the countless stones that were carried along in the glacier. At first the boulder

This is what is left of the glacier that wore the boulder down and scratched it against other stones.

was big and rough, with jagged edges and corners. But the ice shoved it one way and another, breaking pieces from it. The ice rubbed it against other stones, too, and scraped it against solid bedrock at the bottom of the valley.

All this shoving, breaking, rubbing and scraping made the boulder smaller. They also rounded its corners and smoothed its sides. Last of all, many sharp stones were pushed against it. They dug into the boulder, making the deep scratches that now show upon its face.

This went on for many years, till the climate changed again. Summers became longer and warmer, and sunshine began to melt the glacier faster than new ice could form. The melting ice turned into streams that swiftly flowed away. Boulders, pebbles, and ground-up clay were left behind. They settled in piles and ridges that covered the ground as the ice disappeared.

This special scratched boulder lies near the edge of Athabaska Glacier, in western Canada. But we may find boulders like it in many other places where glaciers once covered the country and have melted or are melting away. Some of them lie on bare ledges of stone, but most of them are found among broken, ground-up rocks that were left by the melting ice.

The largest scratched boulders are so big that they weigh many tons. Others are small enough to be brought home and kept in your collection. We often give these small boulders the name of *cobbles.* The best specimens are made of hard

A glacial pavement in Yosemite National Park, California.

A glacial boulder, or erratic, left by ice that once covered the region where New York City now stands.

shale, limestone or dolomite. Sandstone, lava, and rocks of the granitic group generally are too coarse to show scratches plainly.

When we collect scratched cobblestones, we should also look for *glacial pavements.* These are rock surfaces that have been scraped, scratched, and even polished by the moving ice. Some very fine glacial pavements may be seen in Yosemite National Park, California. They are made of coarse porphyritic granite that has been scraped and polished until it shines. Weatherworn glacial boulders are scattered over these pavements.

During the Ice Age, huge glaciers covered the northern United States and most of Canada. East of the Rocky Mountains, those Ice Age glaciers were so big that they are known as ice sheets. They often carried boulders hundreds of miles and then left them when the ice melted. Such boulders sometimes are called *erratics*. Most erratic boulders are made of rock quite different from the beds or ledges on which they lie.

TILL (page 100) consists of the worn, broken, and ground-up rocks that are left when glaciers melt. It is a mixture of boulders, cobbles, pebbles and clay—the same kind of material we see near the scratched boulder in Canada. Large deposits of till are known as *drift*. You can recognize them by their mixture of big, little and tiny pieces, which have not been sorted and rounded by streams.

TILLITE is ancient till that has been packed and cemented into stone. If you ever drive from North Bay to Temagami, in the Canadian province of Ontario, you will see greenish tillite beside the road. With a hammer and chisel, you can break off specimens showing the mixture of pebbles and hardened clay. You may even break out a scratched cobblestone. Although it is almost a billion years old, it looks like scratched stones found near glaciers that are melting today.

Making Your Collection

Most of us start to collect rocks by picking up attractive pebbles. Some are worn bits of clear quartz; others are agates or lucky stones. We also may find concretions worn from deposits of sandstone or shale.

These specimens give us our start, but to make a worthwhile collection, we must get many more. Where shall we look for them, and how shall they be kept?

Since rocks make up the land we live on, we may find them almost everywhere. They are seen in road cuts and ravines, in stony cliffs, and in fields dotted with glacial boulders. Quarries are good places to collect, and so are mine dumps. They often contain minerals as well as rocks. Miners may help you find them, or may offer to sell you specimens which they have collected.

"But," you may say, "I don't live near quarries or mine dumps. How can I get any specimens from them?"

There are three ways to get such specimens. One way is to collect rocks and minerals when you go on trips. Suppose you visit a lake or the seashore. On the way to it you may pass a quarry, a mine, or a cliff of rock quite different from any near your home. If your father knows you are really interested, he will stop the car long enough to let you get some specimens. In fact, he probably will help you collect them.

You may also exchange specimens with friends or with people who live in other parts of the country. They will want rocks and minerals from your region, and will send you specimens they have found. Rock and mineral societies often publish small magazines or newsletters which give the names and addresses of people who want to make exchanges.

Finally, you may buy certain specimens which you need. Many collectors buy "hardness sets," which are sets of the minerals used in the scale of hardness. Others buy sets of rock-forming minerals. This often is better than waiting months or even years to collect all these minerals.

As you become an experienced collector, you will stop picking up pebbles unless they are such things as agates or veined lucky stones. Instead, you will try to get fresh, unworn specimens. For each mineral, you will want one specimen of its crystals and another showing its massive or grainy form. For each kind or variety of rock, you will need a freshly broken piece that can be trimmed into a neat shape. Many collectors like their rock specimens to be about three inches long, two inches wide, and an inch or two in thickness. Things like bombs and geodes may be larger, of course. So may slabs of ripple marks, mud cracks, and other markings on strata.

You do not need much equipment to collect rocks and minerals. Here are the things you are likely to want:

A prospector's pick or mineral hammer. The pick has a blunt end for pounding and a sharp point. The hammer has a blunt end and a flat blade for splitting or trimming. The pick is better for all-round use.

A cold chisel about five-eighths inch wide, for splitting and trimming rocks. Get a larger chisel if you expect to break much granite.

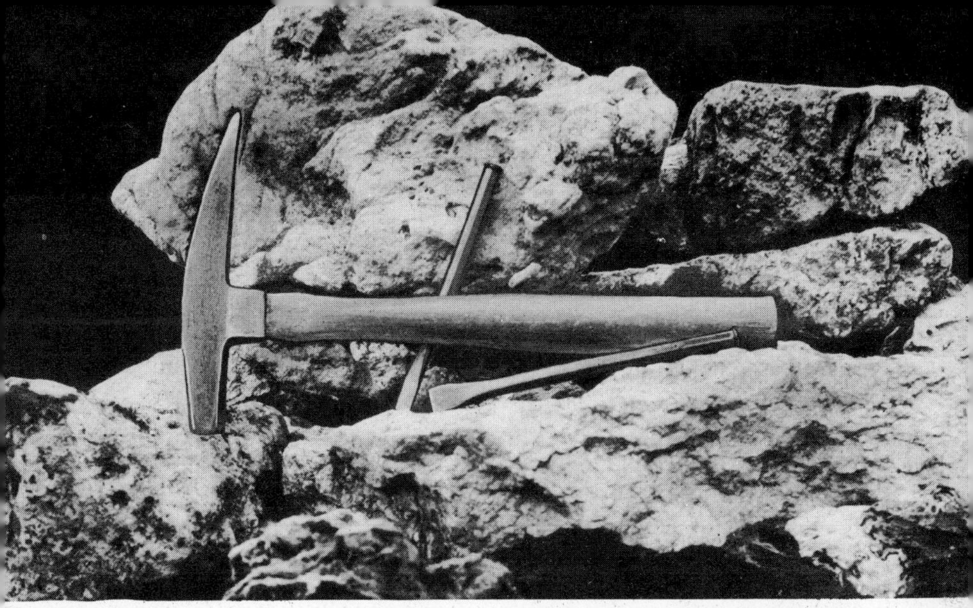

A prospector's pick and two chisels.

Notebook and pencil. Use a cheap notebook for notes about places where you find specimens.

White paper, for labels. Put a label with every specimen, telling where it was found.

Wrapping paper. Old bags or newspapers will do. Wrap every specimen to make sure it does not rub against others, and to keep its label from being lost.

A small, inexpensive magnifier. You will need this to see mineral grains and grains in sedimentary rocks.

A knapsack to hold specimens, notebook, chisel, and other things. Schoolbags are too small and weak for this work.

Some collectors like to carry an acid bottle. Others leave it at home, where it will not be broken. Get a small bottle with a rubber stopper and glass rod or dropper. Ask the druggist to fill the bottle with a solution that is half water and half muriatic, or dilute hydrochloric, acid. Use this acid to test calcite, limestone, and things that look like them. As you know, calcite and limestone will bubble when acid is dropped on them. Dolomite and quartz will not.

Most collectors do not trim specimens where they find

them. It is better to "rough out" good blocks or slabs and carry them home. There they can be trimmed with hammer and chisel. If you find this hard to do at first, practice on common rocks that can be replaced easily.

When you are beginning to collect, you probably will keep your specimens in cardboard boxes or cigar boxes. As your collection grows, you may spread it out on shelves or in an old bookcase. If this becomes too small, you may have to buy or build a cabinet of drawers. They will keep your collection in order and out of other people's way.

Long before you need a cabinet, you will want to label your specimens and make a catalogue of them. Preparing labels is easy. Just cut some plain filing cards in half or trim out neat pieces of stiff white paper. With a typewriter or good black ink, print a number for each specimen, its name, and the place where it was found. The last, of course, can be copied from the label you made when you collected it. If you know the specimen's age or formation, put that on the label, too.

Your next step is to give each specimen a number to match the one on its label. An easy way to do this is to lay strips of half-inch adhesive tape sticky side down on a piece of glass. Then take India ink and write numbers about a half inch apart. When the ink dries, pull the tape off the glass and cut the numbers apart with scissors. Each number can then be stuck on the proper specimen.

Adhesive tape lasts a long time, but it sometimes comes off. It also is not very neat. If you want neat numbers that cannot get lost, get a very small can of white enamel and a small camel's-hair brush. Paint a spot of enamel on each specimen, in a place that will not show too plainly. When the enamel is dry, write the number on it with India ink. Then cover the number with a dab of clear household cement, the kind that comes in a tube. Such a mark will stay on until you scrape it off.

But remember, painting neat dots and marking on them is not easy. Practice before you do it. And unless you can do neat work, you'd better use adhesive tape.

Last of all comes the catalogue. It may be a loose-leaf notebook or one in which the sheets are bound so they cannot be lost. Put down the number of each specimen, its name, and the information on its label. Add other facts if you wish. Many collectors like to tell when they found each specimen, or the person from whom they got it in exchange. Here are some sample catalogue records:

81. Claystone concretion, ring-shaped. Glacial lake clay, about 10,000 years old. Clay Island, Connecticut River, near Ryegate, Vermont. July 5, 1949.

120. Andesite, west of McKenzie Pass, Oregon. Tertiary Age. From a glacial pavement. Collected by Harry Smith. Exchange, June 1, 1950.

165. U. S. Highway 6, south of Red Rock Canyon, California. From a dark pink cliff that comes close to the road. July 2, 1950.

The last record, you have noticed, has no name. That is because the collector has not identified specimen 165. He will do so someday, however. When he does, he will find the information about it safely written down in his catalogue.

Index And Pronunciations

This index gives pronunciations for unfamiliar names and other technical terms. Numbers in heavy type indicate pages on which pictures appear.